ORPHIC HYMNS
GRIMOIRE

Hadean Press Limited
Unit 30, Mantra House
South Street, Keighley
West Yorkshire
Bd21 1SX
England
www.hadeanpress.com

ORPHIC HYMNS
GRIMOIRE

COMPOSED BY ORPHEUS, FAMOUS OF NAME
TRANSMITTED BY THE HAND OF THE ANCESTORS
INTERPRETED IN ENGLISH BY SARA L. MASTROS
ILLUSTRATED BY BRIAN CHARLES

DEDICATION

This book is dedicated to my father's fathers and
their mothers, to the cerulean Aegean, and the great
chthonic mountains whose tips are now called the
Dodecanese.

ACKNOWLEDGEMENTS

So many people helped with this work, both materially and spiritually, that it's hard to know where to start. You all know who you are!

Thank you to all the people who supported this project in its infancy, especially Edward Butler, my first edition editor, who caught many, many embarrassing errors. Special thanks to Erzebet Barthold of Hadean Press whose guiding hand brought you this second edition.

Eternal thanks and my undying loyalty to Brian Charles, my beloved illustrator and bff, whose ikons bring the hymns to life for me, and to my adored co-conspirator Simon Zealot, whose poetry taught me to write and to dance.

Thank you to Thorkild Jacobsen, whose translations of the Maqlû tablets taught me what magic sounds like. Thank you to Mrs. Kindbaum, the best teacher I ever had, who opened the ancient world to me. Thanks to Dead Can Dance, whose album *Dionysus* was the soundtrack to which I created much of this new, expanded edition.

Thank you to Orpheus, with whose words I struggle and love. Thank you to the long line of keepers of these songs, in whose company I find myself surprised and delighted to be. Finally, my heart and my soul give thanks to Hermes Hermeneutes, the Great Interpreter, who gave me my tongue and lit it on fire.

THE ARCADIAN HYMN TO HERMES

Written on a Pink Bus from Mycenae to Olympia

Listen now, as the Muses sing
for Hermes Kriophoros, the Quicksilver King;
Teacher of Teachers, Universal Mind,
Arcadian child of Māyā, divine,
Mathematician, Magician, Traveler, Thief:
Make the pious man doubt. Bring the skeptic belief.
Bring justice in the market and luck for the gambler.
Bring guidance to the lost and inspiration to the rambler.
Make our words be clever. Let our minds be bright.
Grant unearned luck and true wisdom's insight.
Let our tongues be quick, and our feet quick too;
Let our lies be convincing, and our teaching be True.
Send instructive dreams and controllable visions.
Ennoble our purpose. Empower our missions.
And when, at last, our lifetimes end –
Be our beloved guide, and our psychopomp friend.

WHAT LIES WITHIN

WARNING!

WHAT THIS BOOK IS NOT

I love translation because I translate for love. I'm an amateur. I translate a text because I love it, or think I do, and love craves close understanding. Translation, for me, is discovery.
– Ursula K. Le Guin

This book is not a work of scholarship.[1] This book is a <u>game</u> of scholarship, one I hope you will enjoy playing with me.[2] This book is neither fact nor fiction, but something altogether different from both. In the ancient Mediterranean, and in most cultures around the world (but not our own), the essential division of literature (both oral and written) is not between fiction and fact, but rather between secular works and sacred/magical works, which transmit neither fact nor fiction, but Truth. The original Orphic Hymns, and this book of interactions with them, are sacred text. May they be True, even if they are false.

This book is not a literal translation, nor is it intended to be. Lawrence Venuti, the famed translation theorist, distinguishes between two types of translation. The first are those that 'foreignize' the language they are written in by using phrasing or syntax that would be unconventional in the new language. This is generally an attempt to convey the subtle cultural structures at play in the original language. Other translations choose to 'domesticate' a text, by reimagining what the work would be like if it had been originally written in the new language, and with that new reader in mind.

This distinction is made even more fraught when translating magical texts, because of their unique 'voice'. The famed anthropologist Bronislaw Malinowski, in volume II of *The Coral Gardens and Their Magic*, outlines four criteria to distinguish magical texts from secular ones:

> We can tell when a text or utterance is magical, apart from any rubric or any understanding of how their religion works... It is magic if it has the following four features:

---

1 If you would like a scholarly English translation of the hymns, I suggest the 1977 translation by Apostolos Athanassakis (which includes the Greek), or his revised 2013 edition, with Benjamin Wolkaw (which has more commentary).

2 "We dance to grow stronger. We play to finish the Work. The game is all that matters. Please disregard if you're a jerk." From a poem by Simon Zealot.

1. It has a phonology that is markedly different from the community's regular speech.[3]
2. It is sung or chanted, with numerically grouped rhythmic repeats.
3. It makes present-tense statements that are obviously counterfactual.[4]
4. It meets a certain 'coefficient of weirdness'.

In Greek, the Orphic Hymns display all four of these qualities,[5] and I have tried to retain those special features while largely domesticating the text for 21st century Anglophone mystics. This is easier said than done! As Thomas Taylor[6] said, the hymns in Greek, "diffuse their sweets with full-blown elegance" but "shrink like a sensitive plant" at the touch of a translator. Translating poetry, particularly ancient and sacred poetry, requires choices to be made with every word. As my guide for these choices, I have always asked myself "What Would Orpheus Do?"

My goal for these translations is to produce a collection of modern English hymns that evokes in the mystically inclined Anglophone reader the same feelings of immediate, transformative, mystic experience that the ancient hymns promised to their hearers. Where appropriate, I have included footnotes with explanations of these choices, and occasionally with alternate translations. In my interpretation, I have tried to preserve and highlight as much as possible of the original wordplay, metaphors, and mysteries, while rendering the hymns in what I hope is readable, yet still multi-mysterious, English.

In some places, I chose to keep more familiar Greek words, names and epithets untranslated. In other places, I have foreignized the text *by* domesticating it; this is particularly true with the god names, which I have sometimes translated. I've borrowed onomatopoeia from languages other than English (such as 'rish-rush', a Hebrew word for the sound the ocean makes) and invented colloquialisms (such as 'mega-mighty' in Herakles' hymn, which is both a direct translation of the original Greek and also a nod to his superheroic character). Occasionally, I have translated words with their English cognates, even when doing so alters the connotation. For example, a Greek 'orgy' was any kind of group ecstatic (trance) ritual, not exclusively a sexual one, yet I have sometimes translated ὄργιο with the English 'orgy,' while at other times I have chosen words like 'rave' or 'ritual' as translations.

In some places, this means I've added extra context, making the meaning clearer to modern readers. In a few extreme cases (carefully footnoted), my translation starkly diverges from the intended meaning of the original text. I have done this only where I felt that, as history has slowly made her long arc toward justice, the gods would be ashamed to be extolled as they were of old. For example, in the hymn to Herakles, he is praised for putting down the savage races for the good of civilized folk. I have

3 Foreign epithets / magic words / voces magicae / barbarous names, etc.

4 In the hope that they become true.

5 Some more than others, certainly.

6 Thomas Taylor's classic 1792 translation has long been the standard for Anglophone mystics.

amended it to "For the good of all people, you tame savage yearnings". I have made these changes only after deep contemplation and prayer and have footnoted them carefully. The gods live, and their hymns must live as well. If you do not approve of anything in my translation, feel free to write your own lines to replace mine.

The ancient hymns are written in a meter called dactylic hexameter. It is a difficult and clunky meter in English and can sound rushed or angry. Like most traditional English translators of Greek epic poetry, I have chosen the so-called 'heroic verse' (rhymed iambic couplets) to capture the energetic flow of the originals. However, at times, I break the meter scheme for emphasis, a modern poetic convention which is not present in the originals. I have also favored, when possible, homonym play, alliteration, puns, as well as slant and internal rhymes, all of which are present in the original language, and help to add a 'certain coefficient of weirdness' to the hymns.

These hymns are not silent things that lie, passive and unchanging, on the page. They are intended to be chanted or sung out loud. They are enchantments, woven not with ink, but with breath. Because everyone's speech and cadence are different, you might find yourself changing them slightly when you perform them, for example by adding or deleting small words like 'and' or 'the', or changing an 'I' to a 'we', or vice versa. Don't be afraid to play with them and make them your own! When I use the hymns for magic, I often drop the final couplet (the request) and write one appropriate to the specific matter at hand.

On their road to you, the hymns were passed down orally over many, many centuries, with each rhapsode[7] making their own changes. Even in written form, variant texts exist. There was never one singularly correct way to speak the Orphic Hymns in Greek; much less is there a correct way to speak (or sing)[8] them in translation!

7 The Greek word ῥαψῳδός (rhapsōidos) means literally 'stitched of stories'. More colloquially, it meant 'bard'.

8 If you write tunes for them, I'd love to hear them; email me at Sara@MastrosZealot.com!

INTRODUCTION TO THE
SECOND EDITION

MY ROLE AS HERMENEUTES

In the introduction to the first edition, which you've just read, I talked a little bit about theories of translation/interpretation. In this introduction, I want to talk to you about my own method, which I call 'the art of the Hermeneutes'. 'Hermeneutes' is the anglicization of the Greek Ἑρμηνευτης, which literally means 'Hermes-er', and is usually translated into English as 'interpreter' or 'translator', but sometimes as 'mediator' or 'go-between'. My preferred translation is 'Hermes-o-naut'. The English word hermeneutes is singular, but its plural is also hermeneutes.

So, if a hermeneutes is a person who does (like) Hermes, what does Hermes do? I understand Hermes's core to be the *herma*,[9] a type of roadside idol. A herma was most often a stone cairn which mark crossroads or boundaries. Some say that these cairns are named after Hermes, but it is almost certainly the case that he is named after them, and that their name (and thus his) vastly predate the Indo-European conquest of Greece.

Such crossroads altars were ubiquitous throughout the eastern Mediterranean, and dedicated to a variety of gods. For example, Jakob the biblical patriarch sets up a herma on the banks of the Jordan in Genesis 28:18 and another at Bethel in Genesis 35:14, although this behavior is later forbidden in Deuteronomy 16:22. In addition to altars, and memorial stones (as in Genesis 35:20), hermai also functioned as boundary markers and road signs. They are still used in this context on many hiking trails.

In later times, hermai evolved into more elaborate forms, most often solid stone pillars with a face and erect penis. Although these most often represented Hermes, it was not unknown for them to be dedicated to other gods, or to heroes. Few have survived to the present day with their penises intact; as you might imagine, they are a tempting feature for vandals. These 'fancy' hermai were less often used at crossroads, and more often by gates, where they were touched for good luck upon crossing the threshold. The oldest form of Hermes, his essential self, is the Divine Road Sign. A hermeneutes, then, is someone who points the way. Most often, the word hermeneutes is used as either an epithet (divine nickname), as in the case of 'Hermes Hermeneutes', or a job description, as in 'I, Sara Mastros, am a hermeneutes of this edition of the Orphic hymns'.

---

9 In English, 'herm' and 'herma' are used interchangeably. The plural is 'hermai'.

As a human job description, 'hermeneutes' usually means 'translator' or 'interpreter'. It can also mean something like 'guide, 'scribe', 'secretary', or 'aid de camp'. In classical Greece and Rome, hermeneutes were sometimes slaves, but often slaves with considerable power and privilege. In other cultures, the role of hermeneutes is often played by a senior apprentice. For example, in the 4th century *Historia Ecclesiastica*, Eusebius says (of the Christian gospels) that "Mark [the evangelist], having become the hermeneutes of Peter [the evangelist], wrote down accurately whatever he remembered of what was said or done by the Lord, but not in order." Another example is the character of Posca, in the TV show *Rome*, who was the hermeneutes of Julius Caesar. Plato was the hermeneutes of Socrates. Sacagawea was the hermeneutes of Lewis and Clark. Jakob Grimm was the hermeneutes of many women whose names he erased when interpreting and retelling their tales.

In addition to being a job description for a human, 'heremeneutes' can also be a job description for other kinds of spirits. A hermeneutes is a type of spirit who helps people communicate in the Other Place. There are many types of hermeneutes spirits, from Great Hermeneutes (aka Hermes) to angels, messengers, intercessory gods, inspirational gods, oracles, priests, etc. One special kind of hermeneutes is the familiar hermeneutes, a spirit partner who serves as your aid de camp, translator, and guide in the Other Place, while you act as theirs here.

In this book, I am serving as a human hermeneutes, translating the sacred text we call the Orphic Hymns. I am also serving as a hermeneutes by guiding you through their unfamiliar context. I am doing that with the help of my familiar hermeneutes, as well as the aid of Great Hermeneutes.

I encourage you to seek knowledge and conversation of your own familiar hermeneutes. One way to do that is to start off just meeting any hermeneutes spirit, and seeing if you hit off. You don't have to marry the first one you meet. However, in my experience, miracle of miracles, the divine go-between, Great Hermeneutes, is a pretty good matchmaker. In order to help you seek, I have created the ritual below to meet a hermeneutes.

THE RITUAL OF THE COURTING OF THE HERMENEUTES

1. Build a pile of rocks. Bigger is better, but a miniature one will do.
2. Enter magical space/time/consciousness by any method.
3. Recite some hymns to Hermes. There's one immediately before the table of contents. There's two versions of Hymn 28, the Orphic Hymn for Hermes. There's also number 57, specifically for Hermes in his role as a guide of the dead, which isn't entirely on point in this ritual, but will still work. You can look up many others online. However, I also encourage you to write and recite one of your very own, just for you and Hermes. There is some advice on writing your own hymns in Appendix I.

4. Speak from your heart, in your own words about what you want, like this:

    Beloved Hermes, traveler's friend, protector and guide, keeper of the crossroads and messenger between the worlds, come now at my call. Introduce me to a hermeneutes to accompany me in this work, to interpret, guide, and aid me.

5. Next, say these exact words:

    "I ask this in the secret name, known only to true students, which is Enigma Aglossakoan. I ask this in the sign of the forked-tongue stang, the sign of the caduceus wand."

6. While you say that, make the sign of the horns with your left hand, while keeping your right hand on your herma.

7. Hiss like a snake, and pop like a champagne cork:

    "Hissssssssssssssssssssss Pop Pop Pop Pop issssssssssssssssss"

8. Repeat the following until something <u>weird</u> happens...

    "Hermes, Hodios, Mercury, Stone,
    Open, Angelos, Charismaphone,
    Hermes Enigma Aglossakoan."

9. Be friendly, polite, respectful, clever, and shrewd.

10. Remember to say "thank you" and "goodbye" before you leave.

HOW TO USE THIS BOOK

Of course, you are free to use this book in any way you wish. You are even free to leave it on your shelves forever, and never read it, but it and I would both prefer you read it. Books want to be read, hymns want to be chanted, spells want to be cast. I encourage you to chart your own path through the book in whatever way works best for you. However, when I teach the hymns, this is the sequence I recommend:

1. If you began reading this book at the beginning of the preface, and have just arrived here, stop. Go back and pay some attention to the table of contents. Do you know all these gods? Does anyone catch your eye? Whose English name seems surprising? Read them out loud. Whose name caught in your throat? Who wants to be read? Who wants to be chanted by you, right now? Who is reaching out to you? Whom do you love? To whom is your worship due? Who are you afraid of? Take notes.

2. Choose a single god and go read their hymn aloud. How did it make you feel? Were there things you didn't expect? Did you stumble over the words? Read them again. Did you say something that isn't on the page? Pay careful attention to those places; what does the written hymn actually say? What did you change it to? Why? Is there a Mystery within? Read it aloud again until you can do so fluently.[10] Repeat the hymn several times, as a chant. Look into the ikon's eyes while you chant. Once you feel the power settle into place around you, remain silent for a while, and listen for a response. How do you feel? What are you sensing? Take notes. After interacting with any response, go back and read the footnotes and commentary. Do they offer any additional inspiration? Take notes. If anything caught your fancy, do more research on it.

3. Chose an ikon. Trace or photocopy it, and color it in while chanting their hymn. The final stage of your coloring should be the eyes, which bring it to life.[11] If you're a visual artist, consider adapting the ikons or making your own. While the ikons and hymns are copyrighted, we encourage you to transform them into new works of art. Feel free to make unlimited copies for personal use. I often color a new version of the ikon for each use of the hymn.

4. Do you want to try another? Open the book at random and repeat this procedure. Why were you given this hymn to read? What is its message for you in this moment? Take notes.

---

10 I am not a master poet; it might take a few tries to 'catch the feel'. However, the meter and scheme of all the hymns are (almost) the same, so once you get a feel for one or two, you should be good to go.

11 See also the appendix, 'Working With Ikons'.

5. Try several more if you'd like.

6. When you're done opening at random, read the hymn of Orpheus to Mousaios out loud, but DO NOT yet engage in the initiatory ritual (which is designed for people who have already had significant experience with the hymns and are ready to make a permanent commitment). This hymn is different from all the rest in many ways. Compare this hymn to the table of contents. Some gods here do not have their own hymn, and there are hymns for gods who do not appear in the initiatory ritual. Why might that be? What is the relationship of this hymn to the others? Take notes.

7. Next, read through the whole book in any order you choose.

8. Once you have read and interacted with the entire book, if you want to partake in the Orphic Rite described below, set aside an entire night, from just before dusk to just past dawn. Recruit at least one co-magician to join you (via video conference will work, but in person is better).[12] This is not a solitary ritual, although I encourage you to develop your own solitary practice modeled on it, if you like. However, I encourage you to read it, without enacting it, right now. May it awaken your curiosity, inspire your study, and color your imagination.

WARNING: The following ritual can be destabilizing for people prone to mental or emotional instability, particularly those prone to manic episodes. In fact, the English word 'mania' derives from the Greek word μᾰνῐα (mania). Mania is the frenzy of the Maenads (Manic Ones) – the exact force we're evoking in this ritual. If you've <u>EVER</u> been hospitalized with a manic episode, have significant unhealed emotional trauma, or if you have a pronounced family history of mental illness, you probably shouldn't do this ritual at all. Minimally, **DO NOT** perform this ritual without a compassionate and experienced co-magician in the room, with whom you have seriously and frankly discussed the situation, and who has agreed to 'babysit' your first time. This ritual is DESIGNED to trigger divine madness, and not everyone wants or needs that. <u>You have been warned</u>.

---

12 There is a VERY REAL chance this rite, when done in a group, ascends into literal orgy for some people. Plan ahead, stay safe, and don't let anyone pressure you or anyone else into doing anything they don't want to do. Enthusiasm and joy should be the defining character of this rite, and it is not just acceptable, but required, for everyone to find that for themselves, in their own way.

THE RITE OF THE ORPHIC BACCHANAL

Enter into magical time, space, and consciousness by any method. Sink into the Earth, and then into the Other Place. Imagine yourselves in a wild meadow, just before the sun slips below the horizon. Warm Mediterranean breezes caress your barely-clad body. Welcome to the Witch's Sabbat, and the Great Bacchanal. The rite has not yet begun, but revelers, human and otherwise, have gathered, and tension hangs in the air.[13] The mood is pious and solemn. Do not continue until your imagination has blossomed to sensory experience.[14]

In your best Magician Voices, chant the hymns out loud, in order. In my circle, we just take turns around the circle, and people get who they get, but you can choose to have people 'sign up' for individual hymns. Unless you've practiced together, I recommend against multiple people chanting the hymns together; it's hard to manage well.

Begin with Hekate, the Queen of the Liminal, who guards the space between Here and the Other Place. Open the gates with Prothyria guiding your steps. Try to time it so you call Nyx just as the sun completely sets. Don't rush. Take your time with each one. Wait between each, feel the power settle, and listen for a response. If you are moved to do so, speak prophecy in the name of the deity you have just called; let the small still voice in your heart grow large and lively. Open your mouth and let the words out.

Call every god, and open yourselves to them, that they might join your revels. If you feel called to do so, chant the hymn several times. Drumming, stomping, dancing, swaying, or clapping can help if you are having trouble 'catching the vibe'. Scream, howl, wail, cry EUOI and give yourself over to the rite.

For each god, pour out a swig of wine, and drink one yourselves. If you do not drink (as I do not) choose a different intoxicant. It's entirely acceptable to avoid all chemical intoxicants if you prefer. You can dance, laugh, spin in dizzy circles like a toddler, hang upside down until you're light-headed, or even flagellate yourself to trance, but the rites of Iacchus <u>cannot</u> be properly performed if you are in full control of your body. If you're not comfortable with that (and there are many reasons not to be), then do not perform this rite.

---

13 A full moon near the Vernal Equinox is an excellent choice, but anytime is ok. Being outdoors will DRAMATICALLY increase the power, but it's most important that you're somewhere where you can scream perplexing, pornographic, pagan poetry without attracting undue attention, and where you can stumble, bewildered and entranced beyond reason, to a safe place to sleep. The first time, especially if you're alone, I recommend doing it within your home.

14 If you do not have experience with trance work and intoxicated vision-quest, this is probably not the wisest ritual to cut your teeth on. Start with something simpler, ideally with a teacher. Perhaps work with just the hymn to Hekate for a while, with the intention of opening gates both within and without. All that being said, I am broadly a fan of just jumping in and figuring it out as you go. You'll get your hands dirty, and you might get a little mussed up, but you'll get the hang of it. It mostly just takes practice.

Ecstasy, literally 'ex-stasis', requires you to let go, and allow yourself to become possessed. There are many other ways to interact with the hymns, and nearly all of them are correct. Orphism, at its magical core, is about the interplay between divine incarnation (gods temporarily becoming human-like) and divine possession (humans temporarily becoming god-like), but you can certainly celebrate incarnation without possession if that is your preference.[15] *"Many are the wand bearers, but few the Bacchoi."*[16]

The magic trick of Orphic Bacchanal lies mostly in properly timing the waves of trance. I wish I could provide more advice on that, but it's very personal, and can vary from performance to performance. You'll almost certainly have to experiment to find the pace that works best for your group, and that pace will be different depending on many factors, but particularly who is present and where/when you are. Every time you enact the Rite will be different.

As the hymns themselves hint, it is unlikely (and generally inadvisable) that you will make it the whole way through the hymns on your first shot. It's a contest and a game, and it comes with winners and losers. At any point, you can stop working the hymns, and either give in to the revel or go to sleep and seek enlightening dreams. If it's easy, you're doing it wrong, and you should stop. If it's painful, you're doing it wrong, and you should stop.

Ideally, you'll want your ecstasy to build slowly, reaching peak flow around hymn number 30 (Dionysus), and staying in that climactic state until you reach Aphrodite's hymn (56), at which point it can be (but certainly isn't always) advisable to orgasm. From here, your trance should deepen, turning inward and downward. Let Hermes Chthonios (number 57) guide your descent.

The real mystery work begins in hymn number 76, for the Muses, and continues with their mother, Mnemosyne, who in this work can grant insight into your past lives. Spend some time with her, and drink deep of her well. If the sun is not preparing to rise by the time you get to Eos (number 78), you're going too fast.

By the time you reach the end (Thanatos), you should be wrecked. Unless you're a professional singer, your voice should be shot. Unless you're an endurance athlete, your body should hurt all over. If those things are not true, you've been doing it wrong. Dance more. Howl more. More. More. MORE! This is the Great Bacchanal. Don't half-ass it.[17]

As soon as possible after completing the hymns, go to sleep. If you are having trouble sleeping, repeat the hymn to Hypnos several times. Make sure you have water, paper, and pencil by the bed. Expect to be hung over when you wake up. Record your dreams immediately upon waking.

---

15 Orphism's focus on divine incarnation, stripped of its complementary possession rites, was a core influence on early Christianity.

16 Plato, 'Phaedrus' in *Plato in Twelve Volumes*, 1, trans. by Harold North Fowler (Cambridge: Harvard University Press, 1914), p. 62.

17 Of course, you are free to perform the rite any way you wish, particularly when you are new to it. It's sensible to run a few practice sessions before diving in completely.

The Orphic Hymns are also excellent in smaller, less intense group settings. Try going around the room taking turns reading them at your next gathering. In my coven, we sometimes each just open at random and read who we are given.

Once you have enjoyed the entire Bacchanal several times, you might consider the Mousaios initiation. I know it's tempting to skip ahead to it, but you really should participate in the Mystery as a reveler several times, probably at least once with a group, before you seek to become Muse-touched. There's no going back from that.

WHAT ARE THE ORPHIC HYMNS?

The Orphic hymns are a collection of Greek invocation songs (ὕμνος, 'hymnos') from late antiquity. Traditionally attributed to Orpheus, their authorship is entirely unknown.[18] One legend tells that they were written by Pythagoras, a hypothesis I find delightful, but unlikely. In the form they have come down to us, they were most likely codified between the 3rd century BCE and the 3rd century CE, very likely in what is now western Turkey. The hymn to Apollo, I am told, contains some technical music theory that hints at the later end of that range. However, there are several works with strikingly similar themes and styles which date back to the 6th century BCE. Several 5th century commentators, including Plato and Pausanias, refer to Orphic hymns, although these are likely not identical to the hymns we know today. To my mind, the most likely scenario is that the hymns slowly coalesced out of a broader oral tradition, eventually crystalizing into a fixed written form. However, it is possible that there were many written versions, of which only one has survived.

The Orphic hymns are generally understood to be part of a larger religious movement called 'Orphism' centered in western Turkey, but popular throughout the Grecophone world. The famed scholar and classicist Martin L. West says[19] "As for 'Orphism', the only definite meaning that can be given to the term is 'the fashion for claiming Orpheus as an authority'. The history of Orphism is the history of that fashion."

The exact nature of Orphism is poorly defined. It centers on the worship of Dionysus, Persephone, and the Great Mother. Likely it weaves together many strains of myth. Some features are likely indigenous to the Aegean and her coasts, and were already present prior to the Indo-European invasion. It has other roots in Indo-European, Balkan, Egyptian, and Semitic cultures. Finally, it is most strongly informed by a variety of mainstream classical Greek religious practices. There are very few primary sources which speak about what Orphism is; most classical sources speaking about it are actively opposed to it as a dangerous foreign cult. Orphism was politically unpopular in the halls of Athenian power. It was a cult too associated with outsiders: particularly women, slaves, and foreigners.

Orphism wasn't exactly a religion the way we understand that word. However, Orphism does have its own theological viewpoint relative to 'mainstream' classical Greek religion. That viewpoint is strongly colored by its Eastern origins, and focuses on Zagreus-Dionysus, Persephone, and the Great Mother with comparatively less attention paid to the Olympians. However, more than a coherent and well-defined

---

18 I understand 'Hymns of Orpheus' in much the same way I understand 'Psalms of David'; they are 'inspired by the spirit of...' more so than 'authored by...'.

19 Martin L West, *The Orphic Poems* (Oxford University Press, 1984).

set of beliefs, Orphism was defined by a style of worship and ritual – what we might today called 'charismatic' practice, and which the ancients called 'orgiastic'. Orphic rite is that 'orgy' (mystery ritual) whose goal is to be filled with 'charism' (magic powers bestowed as divine grace) and ecstasy (ex-stasis, or what we would call 'out of body experience'). We know little about the exact details of the Orphic orgy, or Bacchanal, and it is important to remember that almost all our knowledge about it is suspect. It appears to have included many of the following features:

1) a female-led, or possibly female-only procession,
2) phallic wands made of giant fennel,
3) torches made of mullein,
4) masks,
5) intoxication,
6) blood sacrifice,
7) omophagia (eating raw flesh),
8) snake handling,
9) free love.

Most likely, every community had its own unique practices, and probably very few included all of the above elements in every ritual.

The most important feature of Orphic ritual, what distinguished it from orthopraxic 'state-approved' pagan practices, is trance possession. "...worshippers of Dionysus believed they were possessed by the god. It was but a step further to pass the conviction that they were actually identified with him, actually became him. This was a conviction shared by all orgiastic religions, and one that doubtless had its rise in the physical sensations of intoxication."[20]

Among the Orphic mysteries was the promise of salvation from death, which I understand as the ability to retain ego-coherence and memory from lifetime to lifetime. That Mystery, like most, is learned only by experience. As mystics (Mystery delvers), we practice dying until we aren't afraid of it anymore. If I could transmit this Mystery to you in writing, I would, but it is essentially ineffable. All I can do is try to remind you of a Mystery you already know:

> When you die, <u>do not be afraid</u>. You have a body, and you have a soul, but you are essentially soul. You will be tempted to forget all the pain, all the loss, all you've learned. Be strong; <u>do not be afraid</u>. Choose to remember. And then you will celebrate among the Mighty Dead.[21]

---

20 Jane Ellen Harrison, *Prolegomena to the Study of Greek Religion*, 3rd edn,(New York: The Noonday Press, 1955), p. 474.

21 We'll discuss this slightly more in the commentary on Mnemosyne's hymn. You can also Google 'Petelia Tablet' to learn more.

A NEW HYMN FOR ORPHEUS

Listen to this tale of the poet most renowned,
Hero and mystic, weaving magic made from sound,
Orpheus, an orphan slave, from ever-blessed Thrace,
Whose ecstatic charismatic rites crack open Heavens' face,
And under peal of thunder-drums, trace a path from trance to Grace;
Redeeming what merely seems and revealing what's been debased.

The Son of Songstress Muse, high priest of all harmonics,
Archaic story-telling bard hooked on heaven's phonics.
Great cosmic voice that opens up the heavenly abode.
Goetic oracle and orator, our hero and rhapsode
Rose swift to fame and fortune for the stories that he told.
He spoke the language of the birds and sang them from their trees.
He sailed the seas out to the east to seize the golden fleece.
He raised the sailors' spirits, and sang the fish up from the seas,
he outsang sirens' serenade, thus besting bitter banshees.

Some say it was at a wedding that he met his soul's true love,
The princess Eurydikē,[22] called 'Justice Wide Above'.
But she was bitten by a viper, and he held her, wailing woe,
As her soul flickered,
     and fled,
          and made its descent,
               into the depths below.
Others say she was immortal, and her descent not deathly loss –
That she is Great Hekate hidden in Patriarchal gloss.

In any case, brave Orpheus sought his love below the dark,
He crossed the river of life and death, the true magician's mark.
With seven songs for seven steps, he charmed his way below,
Through dark and cold and death and lethe into the earth's hollow.

---

22 The more familiar Euridice is her Latin name.

The Queen of Hell fell under his spell, enchanted by the sound,
and found his love, where she lay bound, beneath the ancient mound.
With further songs and spells he charmed the guardian of the dead,
Cracking locks
      and rolling rocks
           that blocked
                where Justice laid her head.

The Queen gave leave to lead his love back up above the ground:
"But, Orpheus," Hell said to him, "you mustn't turn around!"
Orpheus, still young and brash, failed the Dark Queen's test,
So Hekate-Eurydike sleeps on Persephone's blessed breast.
In impotent goetic woe, Orpheus returned to wild Thrace,
And once again gained widespread fame for his voice and pretty face.
But he wallowed in bitter fury, forswearing She who was his love.
He blasphemed the Queen Below and worshipped only Him Above.

He taught his men to oppress women and engage in child rape,[23]
So Maenads ripped him limb from limb and took his pretty face.
With such death, his soul was cleansed; his rage finally abated,
And he came at last to true love's arms, in the Dark where She had waited.
Orpheus died while he yet lived: That's what makes a mage.
He went below and rose again, he paid Hell's steep tithe-wage.
If you would follow in his steps; if you would open up the ways,
Dare to raise Keyholder's torch and seek Wide Justice always.

This secret rite we'll teach to you, if you read his hymns with care,
      And allow illuminating Dark to lay the long way bare.
          Mystery cannot be penetrated. She must penetrate you.
    Climb your way up out of Hell, but
Keep faith with what's beneath you.

---

23 "Indeed, he was the first of the Thracian people to transfer his affection to young boys and enjoy their brief springtime, and early flowering this side of manhood." Ovid, Book X in *Metamorphosis*, trans. by A.S. Kline (Ann Arbor: Borders Classics, 2004).

THE HYMNS OF ORPHEUS

TRANSMITTED BY THE ANCESTORS TO OUR PRESENT DAY

TO PRAY AS ONE OF THE MUSE-TOUCHED

The Orphic hymns open with what is framed as a short note from Orpheus to Mousaios, teaching him a prayer form. The opening lines say: "Learn this ritual,[24] Mousaios. It's the best prayer, certainly excelling all others."

Mousaios is a proper name, which literally means 'of the Muses'. In myth, he is understood to be one of the great ur-bards of ancient Greece, along with Orpheus, Hesiod, and Homer. Some say he is the teacher of Orpheus, and some that he is the son of Orpheus and Selene. There are even those who believe that Mousaios is identical to the biblical Moses.

However, in this piece, I understand it to be a title, rather than a proper name. A 'mousaios', I believe, is one who is 'of the Muses', that is to say, their initiate. This reading explains the function of this hymn in relation to the others, and why it differs in structure. It is the preliminary initiation into muse-craft, so that one might speak with the authority of Orpheus.

If this is, indeed, an initiation ritual, it lacks the explicit instructions we need to work the text. However, by making use of those fragments of the Orphic secrets which have come down to us and interpolating them with several other initiations of the same general time period and culture, we can construct a ritual that I have found extremely effective. The most important text I referenced in this reconstruction is the Derveni papyrus, and another important key was PGM XIII 934-949 (titled 'As the revelator Orpheus handed down in his secret instruction'). Also relevant is PGM III 412-423, which you can find in the Mnemosyne chapter.

In this interpretation, I have chosen to translate the names of the gods into modern English. I made this choice to highlight the fact that this is an initiation into a living tradition – one with deep and ancient roots, but one that that bears fruit in every age. I have footnoted each translated name with its Greek counterpart. More details on the etymology of many of the names are found in the commentary accompanying their hymns.

My translations of these names are in no way definitive; many of the origins of the gods' names are speculative at best, and some are entirely lost to time. This is particularly true of the oldest gods, who vastly predate the invention of the Greek language. If you would like to further investigate the names, I strongly recommend *NTC's Classical Dictionary: The Origins of the Names of Characters in Classical Mythology*, by Adrian Room. It has a surprisingly delightful dry wit and is useful for both research and bibliomancy.

---

24 Unlike the rest of the hymns, which usually refer to the goings on as a τελεται, or 'ceremony', this one uses θυηπολία, which means more like 'ritual'.

THE HYMN OF ORPHEUS FOR MOUSAIOS

I cry out to illustrious God,[25] the king,
And to Earth,[26] firm foundation of everything.

The brilliant fire of Sun,[27] the Moon's[28] glowing shine,
The ever blazing Stars[29] alight in their heavenly shrine.

The dark headed Sea[30] who upholds the Earth,
She of the Grain,[31] and the Murderess[32] to whom she gave birth,

The Great Bear[33] archer, the bright Light[34] of Delphi,
And the New God,[35] the dancer, widely honored on high.

Strong-spirited Man,[36] and Bright-blaze,[37] ever brave,
And crowned with great grace, Foam on the Wave.[38]

And I call that Great Spirit,[39] the ebon king below
Who rules o'er the lands past the river of woe.

---

25 Zeus.

26 Gaia.

27 Helios.

28 Surprisingly, this is not Selene, but rather Mēn, an Anatolian moon god.

29 Astron.

30 Poseidon. Although I have used 'Sea' here, Poseidon literally means 'consort of Da'. Da is another name for the Great Mother.

31 Demeter.

32 Persephone.

33 Artemis. My translation of it as Bear (αρκτος) is questionable. It is most likely derived from very, very ancient proto-Indo-European roots. However, to Grecophone ears, it sounds like arktoi (bear).

34 Phoibos aka Apollo.

35 Dionysus.

36 Ares.

37 Hephaestus.

38 Aphrodite is not called by name but referred to as the 'foam-born goddess'.

39 Hades is not called by name here, but it is surely him.

Youth-Bloom,[40] the Liberator,[41] whose love tamed the rage
Of the ever Glorious Hero,[42] mega-mighty and brave.

Righteousness,[43] Piety,[44] be embodied tonight,
O greatest of blessings, descend upon your acolyte!

I summon the Brides[45] of the wilds, of the forests and the fields
And good Mr. Everything,[46] who's a really big deal.

I call to Air,[47] blessed bed partner and powerful twin
Of the King of the Sky[48] and his shield of goatskin.[49]

Memory,[50] dazzling, delightful, splendid, sublime,
And Inspirations,[51] the mysterious and mystical nine.

I call to the Graces,[52] the Seasons,[53] the Year,[54]
Dancing a circle, I beg you: Appear!

I call to the Hidden One,[55] she of fair hair,
And upon the She-God,[56] precious and rare.

---

40 Hebe.

41 Eilythyria.

42 Herakles.

43 Dikaiosune.

44 Eusebia.

45 Nymphs.

46 Pan.

47 Hera.

48 Zeus.

49 Aegis.

50 Mnemosyne.

51 Muses.

52 Charities.

53 Horai.

54 Eniautos.

55 Leto. This translation is speculative and is based in the similarity between her name and 'lotus' (the flower of oblivion), 'lethe' (forgetfulness) and 'lateo' (to lie hidden).

56 Dione.

I call out to the Youths,[57] wielding fierce spears,
And the Crowns of the Mountain,[58] their warrior Peers.[59]

I call the gods of Mt Ida, the ageless scions of Zeus,
Brazen warrior saviors, brass-clashing youths.

I cry to the Crossroad,[60] the angel, the sign,
And Good Order,[61] telling fortunes for all of mankind.

I summon forth the primeval goddess called Night,[62]
And Day,[63] the light-bringer, brilliant and bright.

I conjure Justice,[64] and also Faith-Trust[65]
And She Who Gives Law,[66] all of them just.

I call to the Flow,[67] cosmic time's outward surging
And her consort, the Claw,[68] the scythe's inward scourging.

The Primeval Ocean,[69] and Grandmother[70] Sea,
Come with all of your daughters, wild and free.

I call the Enduring One,[71] who upholds the mountains
And Eternity,[72] timeless time, forever unbounded.

---

57 Kouretes.

58 Korybantes.

59 Kabiri is probably related to the Hebrew חבר which means 'friend' or 'colleague'.

60 Hermes.

61 Themis.

62 Nyx.

63 Hemara.

64 Dike.

65 Pistis.

66 Thesmodoteira.

67 Rhea.

68 Kronos. The origin of this name is unclear, but I think it is related to κείρω, which means 'to shear' or 'to claw'.

69 Okeanos.

70 Tethys.

71 Atlas.

72 Aeon.

I call Time,[73] ever-flowing, and the River of Gloom,[74]
And gentle Foresight,[75] who grants the oracles' boon.

I call to the good spirits, beneficent and holy,
And also the others, baneful and unruly.

The spirits of the heavens, and of the seas' waves,
Those who wander the air, those who dwell in the caves.

I call underworld spirits, and those of the flames,
I call every spirit, both named and unnamed.

Mother Earth[76] and the Roarer,[77] and all those who dance
In the Bacchanal revels, where we whirl hand-in-hand.

I call in the White Goddess,[78] the savior of ships
And her son, the Wrestler,[79] the bestower of bliss.

I call out to Victory,[80] her voice clarion sweet.
Inescapable One,[81] who hid god in the peaks of far Crete.

I call the Great Surgeon,[82] that all-holy king
Who mitigates pain and blesses with healing.

I call the Spear Brandisher,[83] good maiden of war-cry
And the whistling winds, whip-whooshing on high.

I call to the boom of loud-shouting Thunder[84]
And the four pillars of the cosmos, that gird the world under.

---

73 Chronos.

74 Styx.

75 Pronoia.

76 Semele (see her hymn for more).

77 Bacchus.

78 Ino Leukothea.

79 Palaimon.

80 Nike.

81 Adrastea.

82 Asklepios.

83 Pallas (syncretized with Athena).

84 Brontos (as in 'brontosaurus').

I call the Great Mother of gods and mortal men,
The Dying Lord,[85] and the good Queen of Heaven.[86]

I cry out to Creation,[87] when being began,
And to the End[88] of everything's eternal lifespan.

I call to you all, come full of joy and graceful delight-
Come, accept sacrifice and libation, at this most holy rite.[89]

---

85 Attis/Adonis, the origins of whose name are completely unknown.

86 Ourania.

87 Arche, which means 'Beginning' or 'Primeval'.

88 Peras, which more literally means 'Terminal Boundary'.

89 You may find a new couplet forming on your lips to end this hymn. That means you're doing it right.

HEKATE

Ἑκάτη

1: HEKATE, MAGICIAN

Hekate, Enodia,[90] Trioditis[91] most lovely,
We call to you now, oh saffron-robed[92] lady.
You rule the heavens above and the black depths below.
You skate across waves and flow with the seafoam.
Sorcerous[93] soul, you dance with the dead
And the deer and the dogs who delight in your tread.
Destructive[94] One, Loner, irresistible Queen,
You roar like a beast beneath the moon's gleam.
Unarmored, unconquered, chariot drawn by bulls,
Holding keys of the cosmos and heavenly rules.
Hierophant of the nymphs who haunt the high places,
You nurture children with charm and good graces.
We pray, hallowed maiden, please make our hearts light,
Goddess, indulge your initiates and visit our rite.

It is no accident that Hekate's is the first Orphic Hymn. As the goddess of sorcery and initiation, every liminal space is hers, and she is the gatekeeper of every mystery. In this guise, she is hailed as Propylaea, She of the Gates. The Greek word *propylaeon* (προπύλαιον) means literally 'pro-pylai', 'before-gate'. Today, the word is used by archaeologists to refer to the gated entrance of an ancient temple, flanked by large columns.

Throughout the classical world, shrines and statues of Hekate were placed by gateways: the gates of cities and temples, as well as the doors of individual homes. At Lagina, as well as in Miletus, Thasos, and Rhodes, Hekate had shrines at the city gates.

---

90 'Of the streets'. In both modern and ancient Greek, it can also mean 'streetwalker' as a euphemism for a prostitute, or 'street person' as a euphemism for a homeless person, but I have no reason to believe that either meaning is expressly implied here, except inasmuch as gods of the streets and the crossroads are always also gods of the people who live and work there, including prostitutes, petty thieves, itinerant preachers, prostitutes, and other 'street people'.

91 'Of the three-way' (crossroad). Broadly, in the ancient world, four-way crossroads were only in cities and markets. More rural roads and paths were more often three-ways.

92 'Saffron-robed' (Κροκόπεπλον) is a lunar epithet. You know how when the moon is hidden by clouds, she appears to have an amber aura? That is the saffron robe being referenced.

93 This word (τυμβιδίαν) means literally 'tomb-y'.

94 The word I rendered as 'Destructive One' (Περσείαν) is often translated as 'child of Perses', a titan whom Hesiod presents as Hekate's father. His name means 'The Destroyer'. It can also mean 'Persian'. Personally, I believe that the titan Perses is invented as the father of Hekate to explain her being called 'Persian' once Greece and Persia are no longer friendly.

At the Acropolis of Athens, a large statue called Hekate Epipyrgidia[95] (Hekate of the Tower) guards the entrance.

Great Greek houses very often had small marble statues or plaques of Hekate (called Hekataia) at the doorways. There is good reason[96] to believe that more modest homes also had them, likely made of wood. Such wooden plaques rarely survive the centuries. Hekate's early association with gates and doorways is primarily protective, and helps explain her associations with keys, torches, and dogs as well.

In addition to her role guarding literal doorways, Hekate Propylaea is also a goddess of the threshold between our world and the Other Place. In mythology both classical and modern, Hekate is unquestionably an initiatrix of all who seek to travel between worlds. Like every Dweller at the Threshold, Hekate Propylae can appear fearsome the first time you meet her. This is largely because you (probably) grew up in a culture that demonizes the underworld, and leads us to be afraid of the spirit world. It's true, there are dangers here. Everything worth doing is so because it has the power to change you, and that is a dangerous and scary thing. Calm your fears, and approach Hekate Propylaea respectfully, but without fear. She will test you; her gateway can appear as a mirror which reflects back all the terrible things we think about ourselves.

A SPELL TO OPEN THE GATES OF MYSTERY

You will need:

- A tabletop or other surface, ideally one you can permanently dedicate as an altar
- 1 white pillar candle
- 1 black pillar candle
- A Hekate ikon
- 1 large bowl, preferably silver
- Water to fill the bowl, preferably 'living' water you have collected from rain, a river, a spring, or another natural source, but bottled spring water is also good, and tap water is ok.
- Frankincense resin, although oil will work in a pinch
- Brazier and charcoal
- A head-covering that hangs at the sides, keeping your field of vision small.
- About half an hour of uninterrupted time, ideally at night when the moon is dark.

---

95 Some say this statue was the first to show Hekate as having three faces. More likely, it popularized that form in Athens.

96 Christine Alexander, 'A Wooden Hekataion of the Hellenistic Period', *The Metropolitan Museum of Art Bulletin*, 34.12 (1939), 272-274 <https://www.jstor.org/stable/3256233>.

Arrange your space with the ikon in the center back, and the bowl in front of that. Place the white candle on the right and the black one on the left. Put the incense in front of the bowl. Ideally, you want it set up so that you look through the incense smoke at the ikon, which is reflected by candlelight on the surface of the water. Fill the bowl, light the candles and incense, cover your head, and enter magical space, time, and consciousness in whatever way is your custom. When you are ready to begin, imagine Hekate opening her arms to you as you speak from your heart, saying something like:

> *Hekate Propylaea,*
> *Who Guards the Gates of the Three Worlds,*
> *I stand before you as a supplicant,*
> *I ask entry into your mystery —*
> *Allow me to pass through the gates of initiation*
> *and into your teaching.*
> *I light incense before you.*
> *I pay homage to you.*
> *This I will do each dark moon,*
> *for so long as we both so wish.*

> *Open the gates of my mind to know your truth.*
> *Open the gates of my spirit to feel your presence.*
> *Open the gates of my ears to hear your voice.*
> *Open the gates of my eyes to see your vision.*
> *Open the gates of my body,*
> *that I may fly forth and return again.*
> *Hekate Propylaea, open every gate to me,*
> *and walk with me as I traverse them.*

PROTHYRIA

Προθυραία

2: PROTHYRIA, GATEKEEPER

Listen as we call, oh most blessed goddess,
Many-named daemon, wondrous and flawless.
For those in birth-pain, you grant blessed aid,
Offering comfort and strength to she who's afraid.
O savior of women, kind-minded birth-giver,
You bring a quick labor and help women deliver.
Prothyraea, key-holder, you help those in distress,
You stand at the door, kindly and gracious.
Your breasts drip with milk, oh lover of nurses,
Your heart drips with compassion, oh breaker of curses.
All mortal beings, you brought into the light,
Meeting we mortals with joy and delight.
Great initiatrix, you turn girls into mothers,
And provide growing families with sisters and brothers.
Sympathize with the pangs, and unweave any doom
That shadows the labor or binds closed the womb.
Eileithyia, She Who Comes, attend to the call
Of those in travail, and comfort the soul,
For you turn away sorrow and disperse all distress,
Prothyraea, Eileithyia, great Artemis,
I call you, attend, oh multi-named goddess.
Giver of children, I beg that you bless:
Bring forth the baby, oh savior from death,
Grant the mother good health and the baby first breath.

Prothyria, under her name Eileithyia (Εἰλείθυια) is the Great Goddess of the sacred cave of Amnisos[97] on Crete. From holy Mt. Ida, the river Amnisos splashes down to the sea through a neolithic settlement of the same name. Along its shores are scattered archaeological sites, including Eileithyia's cave. From there, her worship spread all over the Grecophone world, from the French Riviera to Northern India. She is perhaps among the oldest gods of the Orphic Hymns, her origins clouded in the mists of prehistory.

At the entrance of the cave grows an ancient fig tree. Near the tree, a house for priests (or perhaps guards) has been found. I believe, but obviously can never know, that this 'house of men' was the last stop for male pilgrims, when female celebrants went inside. Seven steps lead down into the Earth and then the path gently slopes up to

97 Although they sound similar, there is no etymological connection with the word 'amniotic'. Surely, however, there is a poetic resonance!

three successive rooms. In the innermost room is a rectangular constructed stone altar. The altar surrounds a *beatyl* (βαίτυλος) or 'holy stone,' in this case, a stalactite in the form of the goddess. Here, women offered milk, honey, oil, and wool, as well as votive statues of women, children, and snakes, in hopes for easy labor and safe childbirth.

From Linear B tablets, we learn that more than 3000 years ago, the Minoans worshiped the great Birth Giver in that cave, under the name E-re-u-ti-jaas. In fact, the sacred site's Minoan name, a-mi-ni-so, was the key that unlocked our modern understanding of Linear B. Votive offerings found in the cave imply that the Birth Giver was worshipped from the earliest Neolithic era until she finally succumbed to Christianity and was replaced by the Theotokos. However, locals still call the cave *Neraidospilios*, or 'the cave of the Nereid'.[98] Surely, as you will see over the course of this book, the Old Powers of the Earth are eternal, and cannot be supplanted.

---

98 See hymn number 24 for more about the Naids. In modern context, this could be translated as 'Cave of the Mermaids'.

NYX

Νύξ

3: NYX, NIGHT

Listen now, as this tale I sing,
of Nyx, the dark mother of everything.
'Kypris' we call you, O blessed Night,
Jet-black, radiant, suffused in starlight,
Delighting in quiet, so sleepy-serene,
Cheerful and brilliant, O mother of Dreams.
Lover of revels that last all night long,
You free us from worry, setting right all that's wrong.
You lessen our pains, soothe us when we weep,
You bless us with the gift of sanctified sleep.
You gleam in the darkness, as your chariot flies,
Knight of the Night who benights sleeping eyes.
Terrestrial, celestial, you circle around,
Pursuing spry spirits, forcing light underground.
Next you flee into Hades, for Ananke decrees
that even the most lofty be brought to their knees.
But, blessed one, beautiful and desired by all,
I beg, turn your ear to your supplicant's call:
Come, kindly Nyx, and bless us with your light,
dispersing the terrors that roam the land beyond sight.

In Hesiod's *Theogony*, as well as in Orphic cosmology, Nyx (Νύξ) is one of the Firstborn powers (*Protogonoi*, Πρωτόγονοι), born before the advent of humans. She is the mother of several other gods, including Aether (Stratosphere), Nemesis (Reparation), Hypnos (Sleep), the Oneiroi (Dreams), and Thanatos (Death). In some tellings, she is also the mother of the Moirai (Fates). In some Orphic fragments, although not in the hymns themselves, she, rather than Xaos, is the Mother of Creation from whom all things, beginning with Gaia, the mother of matter, and Eros/Phanes, the father of sexual reproduction, arise.

Nyx lives on the outermost boundary of the universe, far beyond Okeanos, deeper than Tartarus. There, in a sacred cave, she chants oracles. The rhythm of her chanting is the heartbeat of the world, to which Adrasteia (the Inescapable) beats her tympanon, leading the world in ecstatic dance. She is barely anthropomorphic; her most essential physical form is that of the dark veil which is nightly drawn across the heavens.

OURANOS

Οὐρανός

4: Ouranos, Sky

All-Father Sky, of the primordial exploding
Eternal cosmic consciousness, never eroding.
Spin-twirling cosmocrat, as you encircle the earth,
You are the end of everything, and everything's rebirth.
As home of the gods, you orbit like a bullroarer,[99]
Heaven and Hades are both within your border.
Invincible lapis castle in glittering metamorphosis,
You clutch to your heart the inner core of Physis.
All-seeing cause of Kronos, most uppermost of demons,
Listen now as we say your prayer, for the holiest of reasons:
Induct your initiate in mystic existence.

---

99 Bullroarers are very ancient musical instruments consisting of a string attached at one end to a flat wooden rhombus (which means 'whistling' and is the source of the name for the shape). When spun at high speeds, it produces a sort of mechanical buzzing moaning noise like a dying motor. The earliest known examples are from Ukraine and are about 18,000 years old. They were extensively used in the Dionysian mysteries (and many other kinds of rituals all over the world) to promote trance. You can listen to one here: <https://www.youtube.com/watch?v=5PgGDMmBtDg>.

AETHER

Αἰθήρ

5: AETHER, ATMOSPHERE

God of the high-roofed heavens, eternal and indestructible,
Home of the stars and sun and moon, ever incorruptible,
Fire-breathing all-subduer, spark of life ever-glimmering,
High-shining atmosphere, cosmic element shimmering.
Luminous light-bringer, you and the stars shine together,
I pray, blessed offspring: please fix the weather.

Ancient Greek has two distinct words for the air. *Aer* is the thicker air we mortals breathe, which extends up to the clouds. *Aether* is the upper atmosphere, a lighter, brighter, less dense air that the gods breathe. Over time, 'aether' began to refer to a luminous, elemental substance that permeates the entire universe, the medium through which light travels in space.

PROTOGONOS

Πρωτογόνυς

6: PROTOGONOS, FIRSTBORN

O Elder Protogonos, please heed this prayer,
Egg-born, dual natured, you wander the air.
Bull-roarer delighting in fine golden wings,
All-parent who birthed all human beings,
Erikapaios,[100] whizzing and twirling, mighty with power,
You can't speak your secret, so sprout like a flower!
From your dark swirling mists you bring us the light,
All-spreading splendor, scintillating bright,
On wavering wings, you fly world-wide.
I summon you, Phanes, the Sparkling-Eyed!
Light Bringer, Priapus, to you we sing,
Genial, all-prudent, ever-blest king,
Look with joyful aspect upon these rites divine,
Oh priest of the origes, come down and shine!

---

100 Erikapaios is an obscure name. Scholars disagree on its meaning, and struggle to find a
Greek etymology. However, I believe it to be a Grecophone version of the Hebrew godname,
ערך אפים (erekh apayim). When it occurs in a biblical context (as in Exodus 34:6), this is usually
translated 'long suffering' or 'slow to anger'. It literally means 'long of breath' and is used in
more mystical contexts (such as Zohar) to reference the breath of life with which G-d awakened
Adam. This is consistent with several translations that interpret 'Erikapaios' to mean 'life giver'.
The title will later (hymn number 52) be attributed to Dionysus.

ASTRON

Ἄστρων

7: ASTRON, STARS

I call with clear voice to the heavenly lights,
Beloved bright brood of black-brilliant Night.
I call those pure spirits with celestial tones,
Whirling and twirling, revolving heavenly thrones.
Glittering, glimmering ancient ancestral pyres,
Telling time's tales to the sound of crackling fires,
You guide every mortal on the path of destiny,
Revealing our fates, degree by degree.
You watch over the course of the sky-wandering seven,
Who travel your belt among the high heaven.
From heaven to earth, your path is a blaze,
Indestructible, eternal, having bright rays.
Enrobed in the darkness of tenebrous night,
Shine with your sparkling pure wisdom light.
Come to our holy ritual, our very learned contest,
For those noble few who complete it are blest.

The hymn to the stars is unusual in several ways, not the least of which is its very existence. In mainstream Greek religion, the stars usually did not receive cult worship. However, the Orphic mystery cult was not the only star-worshipping cult in Greece; similar elements were present in several of the eastern-rooted traditions, notably Mithraism. The prevailing folk belief in ancient Greece concerning the stars was that every star corresponded to a unique person. All people ascended to the stars upon their death: the heroes as the brightest stars, and lesser people as fainter ones. It was also believed that stars fell to earth on the occasion of a death.

This belief persisted well into late antiquity, although it fell out of favor among the elite. Pliny the Elder rails against it, saying that the stars "are not, as the vulgar suppose, attached each of them to different individuals, the brighter to the rich, those that are less so to the poor, and the dim to the aged, shining according to the lot of the individual, and separately assigned to mortals; for they have neither come into existence, nor do they perish in connection with particular persons, nor does a falling star indicate that any one is dead."

This seeming incongruity, that a star both comes to earth and ascends to heaven upon a mortal's death, must be confusing to those who do not believe in reincarnation. For the Orphics, however, it is easy to resolve. The innumerable stars are the innumerable lifetimes, each of us ascending into the stars when our earthly body dies, and then returning once more to earth in a new birth.

HELIOS

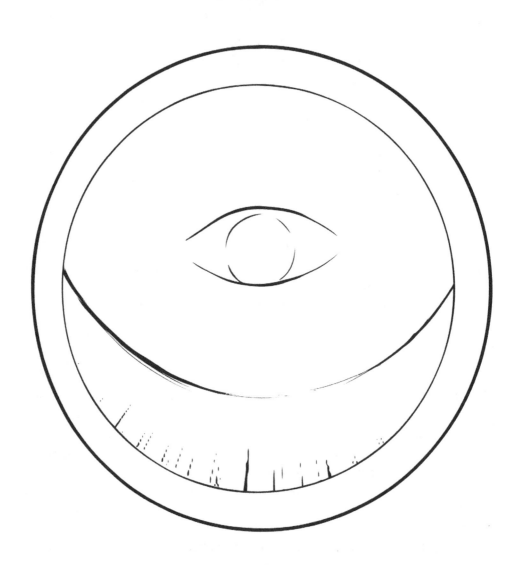

Ἥλιος

8: HELIOS, SUN

Hear me, blessed one, eternal all-seeing eye,
Gold gleaming light, Titan Most High,
You are self-made and tireless, of beautiful form:
On the right side, you give birth to the morn,
While with your left hand you pour out the night,
Compounding the hours, endless alchemy of light.
Your four fleet-footed horses gambol and play,
High spirited coursers leading light of new day.
Whizzing blissful and swiftly, fiery charioteer,
Whirl like a bullroarer on your endless road round the year!
Draw forth cosmic harmony, good guide of the good,
Scorch the wrongdoers, who act in falsehood.
You give the signal, and good deeds are done,
You measure the seasons with revolutions you run.
Multiformed and evergreen, eternally undefiled,
Lightbringer, life-giver, cosmocrat, all-fruitful Paian.
You are immortal Zeus, and undying Father Time,
Truth-doing, all-shining, round-running cosmic eye.
You measure seasons, making sense, giving signs,
When the sun sets, and when you rise up and shine.
Flow-loving cosmic king beaming righteous light,
Truth-guarding all-protector, radiant knight,
Whip-whistling horse rider, life-loving charioteer:
Attend to our prayer, and to your mystics, draw near.

MAKING A HELIOS TALISMAN
Based on PGM XIII 1-313

Helios, the Greek god of the Sun, was worshipped as the Great God in the Dodecanese, particularly at his cult center on Rhodes, where his great statue, called the Colossus, was one of the seven wonders of the world. In the ritual that follows, you'll be enchanting a ring, phylactery, or other talisman (OBJECT) for your own use (NAME). Personally, I like to use fancy golden keys as the OBJECT of this spell. The conjuration is based on the ancient Greek magical papyrus called 'The Eighth Book of Moses', and calls on Helios to open the four quarters of the cosmos, and to cause any locks to crumble into pieces. It is effective at opening roads to almost any kind of goal, but is especially good for opening doors to healing, wealth, and fame.

AWAKENING A TALISMAN FOR HELIOS

You will need:

- A talisman that fits in your hand. We'll call this OBJECT
- Solar incense (I like frankincense + cinnamon + orange peels) and a way to burn it
- A beeswax tealight. You're going to have to balance it, lit, on your head for about 25 minutes.
- Olive oil
- Honey
- Ideally, a hot, bright Sunday afternoon – the weather is more important than the astrology for this ritual.

What to do:

1. Clean and arrange a working space sacred to Helios. Ideally, this work should be done outside, in direct sunlight. Make an offering to your choice of solar charities.
2. Wash your hands, face, and genitals. Wear a white or yellow skirt or robe without underpants (you're going to have to reach up there later).
3. Cover your head. (This is an unusual request in Greek magic, but Helios specifically requested it.)
4. Begin by entering magical space, time, and consciousness according to your usual method.
5. Recite the Orphic Hymn to Helios.
6. Light the candle, saying something like:
   > *"I conjure you, Fire, daimon of love,*
   > *the invisible and manifold,*
   > *the everywhere and the one,*
   > *In this candle to reside,*
   > *never dying, ever shining,*
   > *Aflame, alive with holy light."*
7. Yell aloud: *"Helios Axabyxrōm AAA ĒĒĒ ŌŌŌ I I I AAA OOO Tsavaot YHVH-IAŌ Zagreus the god Arat Adonai Basim IAŌ."*
8. Make the following noises: *TAK   TAK   TAK   POP   POP   POP HISSSSSSSSSSSSSSSSSSSSSSSSSSSSSSS*
9. Pour honey over the talisman. Kiss the talisman, and lick the honey off.
10. Pour olive oil over the talisman. Kiss it, and feel its slickness.
11. Say something like
    > *"I am she of the two cherubim, I stand at the middle of the cosmos, between*
    > *heaven and earth, light and darkness, night and day, rivers and sea. Appear to*

me, archangel of G-d, set in authority under the Holy ONE. I call in the name of NAME."

12. Yell aloud: *"Helios Axabyxrōm AAA ĒĒĒ ŌŌŌ I I I AAA OOO Tsavaot YHVH-IAŌ Zagreus the god Arat Adonai Basim IAŌ."*

13. Clap three times, and then whistle a long shrill note.

14. Take the **OBJECT** in your hands and press it to your chest, saying something like the following:

    > *"I call on you alone, the only one in the cosmos who gives orders to both gods and men, who changes yourself into holy things, and brings existence out of the nonexistent and nonexistence from existent things, holy Orpheus, tongue of Helios. I conjure you, spirit coming into air: By the power of the eternal god enter, inspire, empower, and awaken, this key and let it partake of your essence, for I am she who acts with the power of Orpheus, the tongue of Helios, the holy god."*

15. Uncover your head.

16. Stand with your legs spread, like the Colossus of Rhodes, balancing the candle on your head. Hold the **OBJECT** between your hands as if you are praying.

17. Assume the god-form of Helios of Rhodes.

18. Feel the heat of the sun on your head. Feel the candle there, another shining sun. Feel the sunlight descend through your head, and infuse into you. Begin pushing it into the **OBJECT**.

19. Chant to Helios as seems right to you. I recommend beginning with *Helios Axabyxrōm AAA ĒĒĒ ŌŌŌ I I I AAA OOO Tsavaot YHVH-IAŌ Zagreus the god Arat Adonai Basim IAŌ* and then chanting your sacred **SUN NAME**, and then slipping into glossolalia trance. Continue for at least 10 minutes in this way, pushing solar energy into the **OBJECT** the whole time.

20. Eventually, you should feel the solar power begin to overflow the **OBJECT**, and pool into your belly and genitals. If you require healing, at this time, you can divert some of the solar energy into the relevant part of your body, making a spontaneous chant that makes word play with 'Heal' and 'Helios'.

21. Carefully remove the candle from your head, and put it in front of the idol. If you're not sexually aroused and hot for Helios by now, you have not properly assumed the godform. Repeat the assumption and try again.

22. Pass the key through your legs from back to front, tapping your genitals at least three times on the way. Pass from your right hand behind into your left in front.

23. Say aloud something like:

    > *"Open, open four quarters of the cosmos,*
    > *for the lord of worlds comes forth.*
    > *Archangels, decans, angels: Rejoice!*
    > *For the Aion of Aion herself,*
    > *the only and transcendent,*
    > *the invisible one, goes through this place.*

Open, I say to you, Door!
Hear my words, Deadbolt!
Fall into pieces, Lock!
By the name AIA Ainrychat, who was cast upon the Earth,
for the Lord who Contains All Things,
the Storm-Sender,
The Controller of the Abyss,
The Master of Fire says OPEN!
Open, for Achebykrome commands you!"

24. Say the exact words: "*Helios Axabyxrōm AAA ĒĒĒ ŌŌŌ I I I AAA OOO Tsavaot YHVH-IAŌ Zagreus the god Ara. Adonai Basim IAŌ*"

25. Repeat 8 times.

26. Sit in silence, communing with Helios, asking him how to use your OBJECT, and listening to his council.

27. Ask him for a name for OBJECT. "The god will talk with you as with a fellow god."

28. Remember to say "Thank you" and "Goodbye".

29. Return to normal space, time, and consciousness.

30. Drink some water. You're very thirsty, but you might not realize it until you start drinking.

31. Sleep and record your dreams.

SELENE

Σελήνη

9: SELENE, MOON

Hear us, holy Goddess, night-shining queen
Selene, light-bringer of radiant gleam,
Cow-horned moon, racing through the night,
Nocturnal torch-bearing maiden of light,
Waxing and waning, male and female combined,
Luminous silver-rayed mother of Time,
You love running horses, oh fruitful deliverer,
Joy-giving, deep-hearted, big bliss distributor
Whose warm glowing orb illumines the Night,
All-seeing, ever-vigilant, beautiful, bright,
Full to bursting with stars, O pregnant Moon,
Your warm glowing orb reflects the light of high noon.
The rich quiet black is your eternal delight,
You grant favor and luck, shining jewel of the night,
Marshal of the stars, purple-cloaked, silver-veiled,
lux-lustrous initiatrix, Queen of the Night: Hail!
O maiden, bright Moon, accept your initiates' praise.
And shine on our sanctum with your all-blessing rays.

A DREAM INCUBATION FOR REVELATION
Based on PGM VII 664-685

Dream incubation is the practice of inducing a specific dream before going to sleep. It was extremely common in ancient Greece, and all over the ancient world. This spell gives a short and easy method to induce a dream which answers a specific question.

1. Place a mat or blanket on the floor on which to sleep.[101]
2. Ideally with myrrh ink, write a brief summary of the question or concern to which you would like to dream a solution on a strip of white cloth. (or a piece of paper)
3. Wrap the cloth around an olive branch or wand. (or any other stick; a pencil would work)
4. Put the wand to the left of your pillow.
5. Using a black or silver permanent marker, write the following on the glass jar of a white novena candle:

---

101 I did this once, but now I just do it in my bed, and it seems to work fine. If you are not naturally a strong dreamer, it may be necessary to disrupt your sleep.

OIOΣENMIΓ AΔΩN   OΠΘΩ. BAYBΩ. NIOHPE   KOΔHPEΘ   ΔOΣHPE
ΣYPE   ΣΘPOE   ΣANKIΣTH   ΔΩΔEKAKAΣTH   KOΔHPE   PINΩTON
KOYMETANA. POYBIΘA NOYMIΛA ΠEPΦEPON AΠOYΩPHP APOYHP

6. Speak the following words to the candle flame 7 times, and then go to sleep. Alternatively, record yourself speaking the words, and play them on repeat all night.

> Hermes, lord of the inner world, precious tick-tock heartbeat,
> Circle of Selene, shining sphere of light, butter rich and sweet,
> Square of Reason, who invented all words and speech,
> Mantle-garbed advocate, who hears all just pleas,
> Who whirls on airy courses with golden sandaled feet,
> Holding spirit reins, driving through underworld deeps.
> Bearing the sun's bright lamp, singing with light and heat,
> You give joy to those below the earth, who weep and gnash their teeth,
> For whom the Fates have spun their tapestry, complete.
> You're well-known as the Witching One who sends to us our dreams,
> And oracles, by night's deep dark and day's all brilliant gleam.
> The pains of mortals you soothe away, and all our cares you heal,
> Hither, oh blest one, mighty son, no longer stay concealed.
> The goddess who brings full mental powers, ever true and real,
> By your beautiful form and graceful mind, I beg you to reveal,
> The skill of true prophecy, the signs, and all the secret seals.

7. The flickering of the candle on your closed eyelids will carry the spell into your dreams.

PHYSUS

Φυσις

10: PHYSUS, NATURE

Incline to our prayer and grant us your favor,
Physis, All-Matter, divine Mother Nature.
Much-mechanical matrix of clockwork creation,
Ancient Great Mother, accept our libation!
Celestial Anassa,[102] lustrous and endless,
Indomitable dictator, all-conquering empress,
Almighty mistress of the mountainous breast,
Nursing the world, happy and blest.
Imperishable Protogeneia, exulted of old,
Sung forth by the night stars, their numbers untold:
Silent galaxies whirl on light-leaping feet,
The pitter-patter of matter to time's tick-tock beat.
Pure cosmic mother, unbounded, eternal,
Font of all gods, heavenly and infernal.
Common to all, but uncommonly unique
All-pervading quintessence of all that we seek.
Full-blossoming weaver of natural tapestry,
Self-made and fatherless, poly-mythic majesty
Head of hegemony, life-bearing maiden
Victorious charm-weaver, seductive all-daimon.
Self-sufficient founder of multiverse reality:
Ethereal, material, and abyssal locality.
Bitter to the sinner, but sweet to the saint,
All-wise, all-generous, all-giving, all-great,
Queen for forever, rich ripening savior,
Growth-promoting immortal divine liberator.
Father and mother, nurturing all-fruitful womb,
Giving birth to the seasons, coaxing blossoms to bloom.
You crafted the cosmos and you wove the waves,
Your perpetual motion spins nights into days.
Everlastingly circling, quick-flowing, whirling,
Fluid-formed shapechanger, eternally swirling.
Mover and shaker of every eternity,
Worldly-wise essence, much-honored deity:
Enthroned, scepter-bearing, growling with power,
Mountains rumble your presence, roaring out fire.

---

102 Queen. This epithet is applied to many goddesses in the collection.

All-dominating mistress of life without end,
Future-seeing foremother on whom all depend.
Truly, to everyone you are everything,
And from your immortal being all fates spring.
Good Goddess, Great Mother, we humbly request,
You guide us through life, happy and blest,
Bring every good thing, each in its season,
Peace, health and prosperity, wisdom and reason.

PAN

Πάν

11: PAN, THE GREAT EVERYTHINGNESS OF THE PASTURE

I call to strong Pan, lord of the in-between
Cosmic shepherd who roams o'er field and ravine.
Simultaneously celestial, terrestrial, and marine,
I call to you now, O Pan the All-Queen!
Immortal fires reach out with great greedy hands,
Passion cries for her minister, the great god Pan!
Come holy leaper, spin the circle of seasons,
Goat-legged dancer, possessed beyond reason,
Ecstatic rave reveler, full of holy graces,
You cavort under the stars in the free wild places.
Cosmic harmony singer, delighting in play,
You strum the strange strings that bring festival day.
You write fearful fantasies that move mortal minds,
wending their way, like the rivulet winds
Through the blessed goat pastures where you love to play,
With the oxherding initiates in the sacred springs' spray.
Keen-sighted hunter, who strums strings with the nymphs,
Lover of Echo, all-begetter, give us all of your gifts.
Many-named daimon, hyperbolic cosmocrat,
Light-bringing, fruit-giving, heavy with wrath.
Cave-haunting shaman, true Zeus, holy horned one,
You're the throne holding up Gaia's gargantuan garden,
And Okeanos, unwavering, and his deep flowing seas,
Which encircle the earth, and the life-giving breeze,
Giving rise to respiration, the very air that we breathe
Exhalations giving life to the flowers and trees.
And above their green crowns, in the bluest of skies,
Even the fire-bright light, that all-flaming eye:
All parts of the 'everything' for which you are named,
Each in their place, which you have proclaimed.
Your prophecy transforms nature's very foundations,
You nourish the cosmos and engender generations.
Blessed rave reveler, we pray attend our celebrations,
gifting trance possession and entheogenic libations.[103]
Pan who guides forth from the moment of birth,
Banish gadflies of madness to the ends of the earth.

---

103 The Greek is more literally 'libations walking full of divine frenzy'.

While the Greek word Πάν (Pan) unambiguously means 'everything', linguists say it is more likely that the god's name takes its origin from the Indo-European *peh which means 'to shepherd'. That root is also the origin of the English word 'pasture'. Combining these meanings, I understand Pan to be the god called 'Great Everythingness of the Pasture'.

❀ ❀ ❀

I would like to share with you a dream I had of a life with Pan. The vision is from the perspective of a boy, about ten years old. It is early summer, and the lambs are now old enough to make the trek to the high mountain pastures. This is the first year I have been permitted to join my older brother on this adventure. Brother shows the way to the special meadow, where the most tender and delicious herbs grow. The way to this meadow is a secret closely guarded by our family. With the lambs, we make our way up the steep trail, twisting one way and then the other. We play a tune on our pipes. We come at last to the sacred meadow, and while the animals happily graze, my brother shows me another secret.

We gather the tiny mushrooms of the meadow. They are very bitter and disgusting tasting, but my brother says I must eat them if I wish to become a man. I choke them down. Now he says, we have only to wait for the god to come.

We lie in the warm grass and watch the lambs graze happily on the celestial meadow. We watch the clouds blow through the bright grass. Rainbow patterns shine everywhere I look, a beauty unrivaled by anything I've ever seen. I look at my brother for an explanation, but he only smiles, and tells me that the Great God Pan is in the mushrooms, and I am learning his mysteries.

I cannot lie still any longer. I play my pipe, and the music of the celestial spheres pours out. I dance with my sheep, placid as clouds. I am filled with the knowledge that I am the meadow and the sky and the song and sheep. I am filled with the knowledge of Everything. I am filled with the spirit of the Great God Pan. This is the god of my family, the Great Everythingness of the Sacred Pasture. IO Pan! IO Pan! IO Pan!

❀ ❀ ❀

I cannot say with any confidence that the ancient cult of Pan involved the use of *Psilocybe semilanceata*, the meadow mushroom now commonly called 'liberty caps'. All I can say is that *Psilocybe semilanceata* is common in Greece (and throughout Europe), that it loves to grow in meadows well fertilized with sheep and goat dung, and that (like all psilocybe) the characteristic quality of its intoxication is a feeling of oneness with the Divine Everything.

When understood in this context, the Orphic Hymn to Pan makes an excellent blessing over any kind of entheogen, but particularly mushrooms. When used in this way, the final couplet asks Pan to bless the entire experience, and to banish all 'bad trip'.

HERAKLES

Ἡρακλῆς

12: HERAKLES, GLORIOUS HERO

Strong-armed Herakles, mega-mighty brave Titan,
Competitive, adamantine, strong-minded, enlightened,
Shape-changing Time Father, eternal and kind,
Much entreated with prayers from all of mankind:
All know your story, yet your essence is ineffable;
Your wild spirit untamed and forever unquenchable.
All-dynastic ruler who reigns from the heart,
Archer and augur who never misses the mark,
All-devouring pangenitor, adored protector and lover,
Highest and strongest, bravest child and brother,
For the good of all people, you tame savage yearning,[104]
Firstborn spear thrower, your heart's ever burning
With passion and energy. O daemon great-named,
You wear a crown of night's blackness tipped in starflame,[105]
You bested twelve trials, from the east to the west,
Much-tested hero, ever holy and blest.
Immortal and immovable, immaculate and immense,
Both blessing and healing are yours to dispense.
Come shaking your club to exorcise evil,
Banish even foul death with your weapons primeval.

Herakles is the archetypal superhero of ancient Greece. Like all heroes, he began life as a mortal. He was, in life, called Alcides or Alcaeus (Ἀλκαῖος), from the root *alke* (Ἀλκή), which means 'strength of body' or 'physical force'. In life, he accomplished great deeds, including his famous twelve labors. He then ascended to the ranks of the Mighty Dead or 'heroes' (ἥρως) after his death, acquiring the name Ἐρακλης or Ἡρακλῆς. Many people interpret that name as 'Hera's glory'; it may be more simply 'the hero's glory'. What is unquestionable, however, is that Herakles' story is wrapped up in Hera's, and that his glory is wrested from her.

As the paragon of heroes, Herakles ascended even further, and took his place among the gods. In this way, he dwells in both the Underworld, among the Ancestors, and in the Upperworld, among the gods. Some consternation surrounded him being in both places. Odysseus, recounting a type of necromantic ritual called a *nekuia* (νέκυια), says "And next I caught a glimpse of powerful Heracles—His ghost I mean: the man

---

104 As we discussed in the introduction, the hymn more literally says 'for the good of civilized men, you put down the savages', but fuck that noise.

105 This is an allusion to the zodiac, which is mythologically connected to the story of Herakles' labors.

himself delights in the grand feasts of the deathless gods on high…"[106] While this appears problematic for many commentators, it is very much in keeping with modern folk practices surrounding the Mighty Dead all around the world.

It is hard to know when the veneration of Herakles began. No tomb-shrine has been found that can clearly be identified as belonging to Herakles. I believe this is intentional, and underscores that Herakles, unlike other, more localized cults, is a hero for all of Greece, and all of her cultural inheritors (like us!). His cult is attested to as early as the 6th century BCE but was already widespread at that point.

In addition to being physically strong and brave, at his best Herakles is generous, clever, and playful. However, he is frequently beset by a sort of madness that makes him violent and rapacious. In many ways, Herakles is the mythic archetype of the classical kingly patriarch. This is highlighted by his 'war' with Hera, and with every other woman in his life. When Herakles is an infant, Hera is tricked into nursing him, but he bites her on the nipple. The milk that sprays from her nipple creates the Milky Way.[107] Later, in a bout of madness which Homer attributes to Hera,[108] he murders his children from his first marriage.[109] As penance, he engages in his famous twelve labors. After that, you would think Herakles would have learned the error of his ways, but it was not so. While questing with the Argonauts, Herakles met the princess Iole, who has pledged to marry any man who could best her in archery. When Herakles competes, even though he wins, Iole and her father refuse marriage to him. "After all," they say reasonably, "he murdered his previous family!"

Enraged, Herakles murdered the king and his sons, all except Iphitus, who had become Herakles' lover (the consensuality of this relationship varies, depending upon who is telling the tale). After murdering her family, he abducts Iole and takes her home as his sex-slave, against both her will and that of his then-current[110] wife, Deianira. Iphitus accompanies them. Time passes, and once again Herakles 'goes mad' and murders his lover Iphitus. Seeking absolution, Herakles then spends three years as the slave of Omphale, queen of Lydia, the wielder of the famed axe of power.

The consummate dominatrix, Omphale tames Herakles, and 'cures' him of his madness. After that, she releases him from his slavery, and they marry. However, Deianira and Iole, yet unavenged, send him a poisoned shirt as a wedding gift, which melts the flesh from his bones, and causes such agony that he voluntarily lays down on his funeral pyre. His mortal portion burns, but his immortal half flees, ascending to Olympus, where he marries Hebe, whose name means 'innocence'.

In later myth, Hebe is understood as a goddess of youth, the youngest daughter of Hera. However, in the Peloponnese where she originates, she was worshipped as a

---

106 Homer, *The Odyssey*, trans. by Robert Fagles (London: Penguin, 1997), 11:690-693.

107 Herakles rejoices in many stellar myths, including those of his twelve labors, traditionally associated with the zodiac.

108 In modern terms, I suspect we would call this 'battle PTSD'.

109 His wife at the time is Megara, whom you may know from the Disney movie.

110 The order of his marriages is sometimes different in different stories.

goddess of forgiveness and absolution. For example, freed prisoners, who had atoned for their crimes, hung their broken chains on her sacred trees.[111] I choose to understand this to mean that heavenly Herakles has finally overcome his madness and has been truly absolved. Thus, celestial Herakles is free from the stain of rape and murder, for which chthonic Herakles still atones in Hades. In penance, Herakles is a strong protector of women and children, and can be called upon in any work that smashes Patriarchy.

A Spell to Defend Women, Children, and Others Vulnerable to Patriarchal Violence

This is a serious spell for a serious situation; it calls strong forces, has a high cost, and has life-altering results. DO NOT cast this spell to defend from 'abuse'. This spell is for actually defending from actual abuse. While it is not explicitly written to harm the abuser, that is likely to be a side effect in proportion to the abuse. I recommend against casting it on behalf of others unless you are an experienced magician. Expect significant magical backlash if you go back to your abuser after casting this spell. Work with care.

You will need:

- paper; a brown paper grocery bag is ideal
- pen or pencil
- matches or a lighter
- a toilet
- about 8 minutes of fully suspended disbelief

Things it's nice to have:

- a printout of the Herakles ikon
- a red pen
- a picture of the abuser
- a red candle, and a way to light it
- a toilet
- about 30 minutes of fully suspended disbelief on a Tuesday after dark

---

111 Pausanias, *Description of Greece* 2. 13.4 Pausanias, *Description of Greece: A Pausanias Reader*, trans. by Gregory Nagy, (2020), *The Center for Hellenic Studies*, <https://chs.harvard.edu/description-of-greece-a-pausanias-reader/> [accessed 30 July 2022].

Things to make it fancy:

- a Herakles ikon you colored while focusing on the work
- dragon's-blood ink and a steel-nibbed pen
- the abuser's hair or other body part/fluid
- an oil lamp burning chili oil
- a swamp
- fully suspended belief in the last hour of Saturn on the day of Mars

What to do:

1. Begin by calming your mental chatter and suspending your disbelief.
2. Write the victim's name behind Herakles (either on the back of the ikon, or else just write the victim's name, and then write Herakles' name (in English and Greek) over the top.
3. Write the abuser's name on the back of their photo (or just write it nine times on a piece of paper). Think clearly and in detail about how they hurt you, and how you fear they might hurt you in the future. Put your pain into the paper. Put your fear into the paper. Put all of your feelings into the paper. Put all that you can of your abuser into the paper.
4. Read the Orphic hymn to Herakles, preferably out loud, and then address Herakles directly. Speak from your heart in your own words, saying something like:

   "Herakles, you were an abuser, but you labor to make that right. As a condition of your penance, I call you to defend me!"

5. Repeat "I call you to defend me!" over and over until either your voice or your ability to suspend disbelief fails.
6. Burn the piece of paper over the toilet, and flush away the ashes.
7. As soon as possible, and before you go to sleep, wash yourself carefully from head to toe. Finish by pouring salt water over your head.

KRONOS

Κρόνος

13: KRONOS, CUTTER

Evergreen king, holy father of both gods and men
Wily-minded, undefiled, strong, valiant Titan
Who devours all things, but resurrects them as well:
You hold fast the whole cosmos with your binding spell.
Kronos of Aeons, O Kronos the All-Father,
Your stories are changeable, confounding the scholars.
You're the sproutling of Earth and the star-spangled Sky,
You give birth to all growth and you make all things die.
Cruel consort of Rhea, from whom all things Flow,
The whole cosmos is founded on your dwelling below.
With Promethean foresight you steer past all obstruction
And your crooked counsel is most clever instruction.
We beg, hear our voice, and attend to our cry,
Grant a long blameless life, until our time to die.

Kronos' name has a complicated etymology. Although by the time the hymns were written, Kronos (Κρόνος) had been fully syncretized with Chronos (Χρόνος), Father Time, the two were originally distinct gods. The ancients often derived Κρόνος (Kronos) from *koros* (κόρος which means 'satiety'. This connects to Saturn's name, who, as Cicero says, "is saturated with years". However, many modern scholars prefer to derive it from *keiro* (κείρω) which means 'to cut or claw', for his famous sickle, with which he cuts down both the yearly harvest and his father's genitals.

Kronos is perhaps most important in his role as the spirit of the Golden Age, the first of the five traditional mytho-historical eras by which the classical world understood its origins. In *Works and Days*, Hesiod gives one of the earliest surviving accounts of these 'ages of man'. There is some reason to believe that this was based on an older tradition from Asia Minor and greatly reworked by Hesiod to accurately reflect history as he knew it. Noted classicist J. Gwyn Griffiths writes: "The transition from myth to history is so skillful and so unconscious that we at first hardly realize that Hesiod is giving us a piece of true tradition about the Mycenaean Age."[112]

According to Hesiod, the first phase of history is the Golden Age, a peaceful pastoral era. In this time, gods and men walked side by side. The ancestors of this era live on as guardian daemons, "kindly, delivering from harm, and guardians of mortal men; for they roam everywhere over the earth, clothed in mist and keep watch on judgements and cruel deeds, givers of wealth." Hesiod tells us that during this time, food was abundant: "…fruitful earth unforced bare them fruit abundantly and without

---

112 J. Gwyn Griffins, 'Archaeology and Hesiod's Five Ages', *Journal of the History of Ideas*, 17.1 (1956) <https://doi.org/10.2307/2707688> [accessed 26 July 2022].

stint. They dwelt in ease and peace upon their lands with many good things, rich in flocks and loved by the blessed gods."[113]

From this, I understand him to be speaking, with poetic license, about a span sometime between 11,000 BCE (when sheep and goats were domesticated) and approximately 7000 BCE (the so-called 'Neolithic Revolution' and the beginning of wide-scale plough agriculture).

The Golden Age ended when Kronos was overthrown by his children: Zeus, Hera, Poseidon, Demeter, Hades, and Hestia. As a god of time, Chronos saw that coming, and, in attempt to avert his fate, swallowed his children as they were born. This plot was foiled when Rhea, acting in concert with her mother Gaia, tricked Kronos into swallowing a stone instead of Zeus. Upon reaching adulthood, Zeus tricked Kronos into vomiting up his siblings.

After they were released, the Olympians, as their parents had done before, made war on their father and toppled his government. As the leaders of the rebellion, Zeus, Poseidon, and Hades assumed co-rulership over the three worlds: Aerial, Marine, and Terrestrial. According to one delightful legend, they then drew lots to determine who would become ruler of each world. Zeus became king of the Air, and all within it (anything that breathes). Poseidon took control of the Seas and everything in them. And Plouton, or Hades, became lord of the Earth and everything inside it.

---

113 Hesiod, 'Works and Days' in *Hesiod, The Homeric Hymns and Homerica*, trans. by Hugh G. Evelyn-White (Cambridge: Harvard University Press, 1914), pp. 109-201.

RHEA

'Péa

14: Rhea, Flow

Queen Rhea, daughter of the shape-changing First Born,
Good frenzy loving maiden, to whom oaths are sworn,
Your drum drips with zills, sounding brass in the silence,
And your sacred chariot is pulled by bull-killing lions.
You took Kronos to bed, blest and beautifully formed,
birthed Zeus, Aegis bearer, the high Olympian lord.
All-Mother Rhea, strong-hearted in war-thunder,
You rejoice in high mountains and in making men shudder.
Sneaky savior, who delivered our ancestors of old,
Mother of humans and gods and of all you behold,
From you came wide Earth, and the Heavens above
And the swift ocean winds, whom all the waves love.
In your ethereal form, shaped like the air,
Come, blessed goddess, and free us from care,
Gentle-minded liberator, bring peace, wealth, and mirth
banish filth, gloom, and doom to the ends of the earth.

ZEUS

Ζεύς

15: ZEUS, SKY GOD

To Zeus the undying we sing out this prayer:
Much-honored king of the gods of the air,
You rule over wonders and blessings diverse:
Your wind rustles the trees of great Mother Earth,
Your rivers rush, crashing, to the great ocean lord,
And stars glitter in the heavens on your holy word.
Kronian Zeus, wielding a staff of pure lightning,
Descending in clouds of clamorous thundering.
Beginning of everything and the ultimate end,
Earth-shaker, cathartic one, to our call please attend:
You who wield lightning and nourish the thunder,
You light up men's hearts with fulminous wonder.
Shapechanger eternal, please heed our call,
Grant health, wealth, and peace. Forever. For all.

HERA

Ἥρα

16: Hera, Air

Lapis blue robes enfolding the sky,
Hera, the All-Queen, Zeus' true ally.
Every moment you fill us with sustaining breath,
Giving life to all mortals, from birth until death.
Mother of the clouds, wet-nurse of the gale,
You blow up the storms and give life to the sail.
You alone bring life to the creatures of earth,
You nurture the egg, and you bring it to birth.
You are queen over everything under the sky
And so, with a whooshing, wind-whipping cry,
You roil the waters and rattle the leaves.
Many-named Goddess, we beg you, now hear our pleas,
All-Queen, most blest, to our prayers be inclined:
Be beneficent, joyful, gracious, and kind.

Hera, an Elder God made New

Perhaps more than any other Olympian, Hera's myth and cult are difficult to disambiguate from centuries of political propaganda. Our culture tries to tell the story that Hera is most relevant as Zeus' wife. However, her oldest strata has nothing to do with Zeus at all. For example, at her 10th century sanctuary on Samos, she does not appear to be linked to Zeus, or any of the other Olympians whatsoever. There are strong suggestions that the people of Samos understood Hera to be their divine progenitor. Zeus' conquest over Hera at Samos appears to occur in the late 7th century; this explains why Homer so vicious in his anti-Hera polemic. When the Homeric stories were being developed, she had not yet been fully subdued.

In her old form, Hera is unquestionably the great and fecund Earth, the lady of the chariot drawn by lions, the Potnia Theron, or Mistress of Beasts. In the earliest stages of her cult, the most common offerings appear to have been pomegranates, pinecones, and poppy heads, as well as votives of the same in clay and ivory. After she is subdued by Zeus, pomegranates disappear from her offerings. Pomegranates are abortifacients, and, particularly when paired with a spring/fertility goddess like Hera or Persephone, almost always indicate women's rule of reproduction. When she became Zeus' wife, she lost sovereignty over her own fertility, and was instead husbanded like Cow who became her symbol, replacing mighty Lion.

Even her name is cloaked in mystery; Ἥρᾱ (Hera) is of questionable etymology. Many people associate it with *ora* (ὥρα), which can mean 'season' or 'hour' or 'moment'.[114] Others relate it to *heros* (ἥρως),[115] which means 'hero' or 'mighty dead'. However, many (including Plutarch and I) understand it as *aer* (ἀήρ), or simply 'air'. As we discussed in Aether's chapter, Greeks used two different words for the air. Aηρ (Aer) refers to the regular air that we breathe. The realm of the air extends to the clouds. Past that is the αιθηρ (aether) which is usually translated as 'upper atmosphere'. Hera is the goddess of the Air.

Hera is the motivator of the archetypal hero, Heraklese. Although often presented as punishing Herakles, I understand her instead to be testing him. When he finally passes all of her tests, he is elevated to Olympus and married to Hebe (Vigor), Hera's youngest child. In the first war in heaven, Gaia plotted with her youngest child (Kronos) to overthrow her husband (Ouranos). In the next war, Rhea plotted with her youngest child (Zeus) to overthrow her husband (Kronos). In the current war, is Hera plotting with her youngest child (Hebe) to overthrow her husband (Zeus)? Perhaps only time will tell.

---

114 See hymn 43, for the Horai, for more details.

115 The word Ἥρως (hero) comes from an ungendered root. Over time, as Greek culture shifted and women could no longer be heroes, a new word came into existence, ἡρωΐς (heroine), which by the 11th century CE (the ascendency of Polaris) had become ηρωΐδα (heroida), whose stream is one current that, by the 19th century, coalesced into the Italian witch queen Aradia.

POSEIDON

Ποσειδῶν

17: POSEIDON, CONSORT OF DA

Look, there! On the horizon, where the sea meets the land,
That dark gleaming horseman, brazen trident in hand?
That's Poseidon, who dwells in the deep-seated sea:
Loud-thundering lord, attend to our plea!
You're named 'Consort of Da', the ancient Great Mother,
For you uphold the earth like a tender-armed lover.
When you and your brothers divvied up spoils,
You won for your part the watery roils.
So you came to the depths of the wide-breasted sea,
as lord of the ocean, Earth-Shaker, resounding with glee.
Whipping up waves that rish-rush, crash, beat
Flow, froth, and foam under your horses' feet.
Whizzing o'er the waves and shaking the brine,
Master of the Waters, O Poseidon divine,
You gladden at swells, and beasts underwater,
Oh daemon of the deep, attend to your daughter!
I pray, still earthquakes, and calm tidal waves,
Bring peace, health, and happiness
and lead wealth to the brave.

Poseidon is a very ancient god, likely older than the Greek language. For this reason, it is difficult to know the exact origins of his name. Some translate it, as I did in the Mousaios invocation, as 'Consort of Earth'. Others prefer 'Lord of the Waters'. Still others contend it has roots in the largely lost, possibly legendary, indigenous language of the region, sometimes called Pelasgian. What we can say with certainly is that Poseidon has been an extremely important god in the Aegean since time out of mind, and continues to be so today. Although we often think of him as exclusively a sea god, in ancient days he was understood to have at least some control over all earthly waters. For example, under the title *Themeliouchos* (Θεμελιούχος), which means 'upholding the foundations', Poseidon was closely associated with sophisticated drainage canals to prevent landslides and flooding from heavy rains. In fact, there is reason to believe that Poseidon began life as a god of literal gaps: springs, chasms, and earthquakes. In this role as a god of floods, Poseidon is most often paired with Demeter. Their relationship is tense; he is the inundation that fructifies the field, but also the storm that pelts grain into the mud.

When he is the lover of Demeter, they are often both Horses. All over Greece, Poseidon is praised as the creator of both mortal horses and magical winged horses like Pegasus. In Arcadia, horse-formed Poseidon is the father of Demeter's beloved daughter, the Queen of the Underworld. At Eleusis as well, he is worshipped as the Great Father, and it is this face that most resonates for me.[116]

Although he can be quick and fierce in anger, I find Poseidon to be immensely loving and generous as well, and it is his generosity, and deep fatherly love for us all, which shines most strongly in his modern incarnations. Across the Grecophone world, Poseidon was once celebrated and feasted in the cold, with a "ritual business, marked by jollity and license, [that] belongs to the general type of solstice festival known the world over".[117] He still is, although you have to look carefully to see him. Today, when the sacred signs and symbols of many gods have been appropriated by Christian saints, Poseidon is very closely associated with Saint Nicholas of Myrna. For example, in Argolis, Pausanias tells us, there once stood a great temple to Poseidon. Today, that site is a cathedral of St Nikolaus. In Sozopol, Bulgaria the church of St Nikolaus is right next to Poseidon's ancient altar. Although his actual history is difficult to confirm, St Nicholas' hagiography tells us that he was a 4th century bishop in Myra (modern Demre, Turkey). He was famed for his charity and gifts to the poor, and it is this feature for which he is now known worldwide as the much-beloved Santa Claus.

---

116 Poseidon was my late father's patron among the Greek gods.

117 Noel Robertson, 'Poseidon's Festival at the Winter Solstice', *The Classical Quarterly*, 34.1 (1984), 1-16.

PLOUTON

Πλούτων

18: PLOUTON, RICH ONE

O strong-minded one, who dwells down below
In a deep-shaded glen, black stygian meadow,
O Underworld Zeus, from your throne of black gneiss[118]
throw open your arms and receive sacrifice!
Pluton, wealth-giver, you bring profits to birth,
Wielding the rod of power, and the keys of the earth.
You played lots o'er the worlds, and won the third part:
The abode of the Dead; the Earth's innermost heart,
The seat of the gods, support of mortal men
Where your throne rests in deep, dusk-shadowed fen.
Far-reaching, untiring, unjudged and inert,
You rest, ever breathless, down deep in the dirt
Hades: deep place, great god, dark river of Woe,
You water the roots of Earth deep below.
You accept all of the fallen into your peaceful bed,
For you rule over both death and also the dead.
In the guise of Euboleus, called 'the good guide',[119]
You took Deo's pure child as your chosen bride.
Through meadow, o'er mountain, down through the sea,
Rode your four coursing chargers, gleaming like ebony.
Through the sepulchral path of the Ploutonion cave
In Eleusis, in Attica, at the gateway to the grave,
Kore came to the dark as your chosen Queen,
Singular judge of all things, both hidden and seen.
Pantokrator, all-hallowed by splendid oblation,
Come rejoice in our rites and in reverent libation.
I summon you Holy One, to your mystics' ritual,
Come propitious and blest, kindly and spiritual.

Plouton is another name for Hades; it means 'the wealthy one'. Traditionally, Hades is the firstborn son of Gaia by Kronos, after his three sisters. This means he was the last of the three brothers reborn from the stomach of Kronos. In our culture, we tend to think of him simply as the king of the dead, but he is much more than that. He is god of everything inside the earth.

In ancient Greek culture (as in many other cultures) all life is understood to arise from the earth at birth and returns into it at death, just as annual plants do. This means

118 Gneiss is a kind of rock, similar to granite.
119 Euboleus means more literally 'good counselor'.

that, by ruling over the interior of the earth, Plouton was the ruler of the dead and also the source of the abundance of the fruits of the earth. Additionally, precious metals, gems, and other materials all come out of the earth. Plouton is the god of wealth because all wealth is the spoils of the earth.

Our ikon shows Plouton enthroned, wearing a modius crown and holding a stang. The modius crown is traditional in iconography of Plouton and other gods of Eleusis, as well many related Egyptian gods, such as Serapis and Great Mother Mut. It is thought to represent a grain measure. They are often ornamented with sheaves of grain or a rearing cobra. The stang, or bident, is Hades' traditional weapon. The skull on it represents his rulership over the land of the dead.

This hymn and ikon are an excellent choice to use with most kinds of wealth-related work.

KERAUNION ZEUS

Κεραυνίου Διός

19: KERAUNION ZEUS, THUNDERING GOD

Father Sky:[120] you drive sublime lines fiery bright.
Cut through the cosmic ether, lofty and light.
Crack! goes the lightning across the wide sky.
Boom! goes the heavens' thunderous cry,
Shaking the seats of the all-blessed high gods,
Shattering crack from your blasting rod.
Flowing all-cloudy, the dark looming skies,
Are set alight to the sound of echoing cries.
Lightning flash! Scorch! Set the heavens alight,
Tempest, blow! Storm, thunder! Lightning, burn bright!
Intoxicated blaze, you make all men shudder,
Strong-spirited, quick leaping, enflaming cloud cover.
Your fierce feathered weapons, marv'lous & clever,
Heat-raising, hair-stirring, loud-roaring weather.
Thunder-whistle bullet quick-whirling:
Zeus, unforeseeable, is lightning-hurling.
Unavoidable, unbroken, unconquered, unbound,
All-devouring downpour, loud-pounding sound
Heavy-spirited and sullen, dark-clouded hurricane
Ouranian bullet,[121] sharp falling shrapnel of rain,
Thundering down, igniting both land and seas,
Crashing and clamoring, frightening beasts,
Sparkling radiant in the face of the gods of the air,
Sunder divine robes, and lay heaven bare!
Glittering, glancing, cleaving cannonade,
Electric passion swells seas into wanton waves.
The mountainous peaks know your tumescent glory,
Strong spirited blessed one, spare us your fatal fury,
Accept our libations, and grant pains' surcease,
A heart-gladdening life, children who grow up in peace.
Crown us with honor and luxuriant wealth,
Bountiful thoughts, and Her Majesty's own health.

---

120 Zeus Pater.

121 The Greek says βέλος, which means 'projectile weapon', particularly the kind we call a bola. However, despite the similarity in sound, our word bullet is not related to the Greek βέλος.

ASTRAPAIOS ZEUS

Ἀστραπέως Διὸς

20: Astrapaios Zeus, Lightning Hurler

Blessed one, loud thundering one, listen to my prayer,
Misty, fiery, flashing, shining in the air:
You hurl the lightning, blazing through the cloud,
Clattering as it travels, clashing voice all loud.
God of awe, god of lightning, All-Father, Great One,
Shudder-inducing, heavy with wrath, never outdone,
I beg you: wish me well and banish all strife,
Be with me now until the end of my life.

NEPHELE

Νεφέλη

21: NEPHELE, CLOUDS

O morning breeze, driving clouds through the sky,
Heavy laden and pregnant with rain from on high.
Mist trailing behind you, grey cloaked and sublime,
You bring blossoms to fruit and ripen the vine.
Fiery with lightning and loud-shouting with thunder,
From deep in your folds are born storm and wonder.
Spasmodically blowing, whistling, sparkling with dew,
Your cool gentle breezes breathe life anew.
I pray to you now, bring rainstorms forth,
To ripen the fruits of our mother the Earth.

TETHYS

Τηθύς

22: TETHYS, SEA

Tethys, Grandmother, bright-eyed bride of the Sea,
Whirling and surging, cloaked in aquamarine.
You whisper sweet nothings as you rish-rush to shore,
And crack open the rocks with your waves' mighty roar.
When the weather is calm, you are kind and serene,
Plotting comfortable courses across the wide green
For the glorious ships that crisscross the Earth,
And the free-floating foam of Aphrodite's blest birth.
Your daughters are queens of fresh flowing springs.
Your sons are the thousands of great river kings.
I call you, All-Mother, revered benefactress,
Give fair winds, and calm seas, and our seafarers bless.

Tethys, the first-born daughter of Gaia and Uranus, is an obscure goddess of fresh water, fertility, and nursing. Her name means 'grandmother' or 'wet nurse' or more generally 'other mother'. She is the mother of all water on earth – springs, rivers, underground aquifers, even rainclouds. To my mind, her most archetypal form is as the great fountain at the center of the world, from which flows the four rivers of paradise. She is the Wellspring of Life, and from her fertile womb poured forth the first creatures on earth. In ancient days, before humans walked the planet, she was married to Okeanos. He ruled the salt water and she the fresh. The great river deltas are thus the symbol of their sexual union, and they frequently had temples located in such locations.[122]

So fertile was their union that they had to separate, lest their waters flood all of creation. Okeanos retreated to the edges, becoming the great waters above, the river who encircles the world. Tethys became the goddess of the waters of the earth, and particularly of the waters below, of aquifer and spring, well and hollow. It is for this reason she is hidden, but do not mistake her introversion for unimportance.

The overwhelming majority of the world's fresh, liquid water is under the ground. There is a hundred times more fresh water below the earth than in all of our planet's lakes and rivers. Anywhere you stand, there is water below you. The water may be close to the surface, making the ground swampy, or it might be hundreds of miles below you, but there is, assuredly, water beneath your feet. The shallow waters are mostly 'young', having fallen to earth as rain within the last few months, while the deep waters might have spent thousands of years beneath the earth, winding and weaving

---

122 For example, Alexander of Macedon erected a great temple in their honor at the delta of the Indus.

their way through stone. And yet, everywhere, there is water below your feet. There is no place that Tethys isn't.

In Greece, as elsewhere on earth, underground water is understood to be deeply powerful, healing, and transformative. These waters are the womb of Tethys, and they are among my favorite waters with which to work magic. Many moderns will tell you that Tethys had no cult in Greece, but they are wrong. She had a thousand, thousand cults; the cult of Tethys is the cult of every holy hole and every hallowed hollow.

NEREUS

Νηρεύς

23: NEREUS, FATHER OCEAN

Nereus, you rule from below the loud-crashing waves,
With your fifty fair daughters[123] who all bear your name,
Dancing together within your dark gleaming keep
Midst the roots of the sea, in the heave-seething deep.
O great-named daemon, from ocean floor you give birth;
You are the origin of all and the ends of the earth.
You engender the winds with your generous breath,
Giving rise to the climate from your tempest-tossed depths,
From the gentlest breeze that sighs in your wake,
To hurricane gales that make Demeter's shrines shake.
At the bottom of the ocean, please hold out your hand,
And still seismic shaking that shudders the land.
Please bless your mystics with peace and great wealth,
And the happy serenity of all-soothing health.

---

123 The Nereids. See hymn 24.

NEREIDS

Νηρηῐδες

24: Nereids, Daughters of the Ocean

Pure nymphs of Nereus, faces pink like anemone,
Dancing deep gleeful paths on the floor of the sea,
Fifty fine daughters surrounding the swells,
Dionysus' darlings clad in seaweed and shells.
In Triton's grand chariot, you rise to the surface,
Bestial, primal, beautiful, glorious.
Deep-dwelling daughters of divine Pontos' seed,
Leaping and whirling, riding dolphins as steeds.
Surfing the waves in the violet dawn's light,
You were the first to teach us this mystery's rite.
You bestow holy wisdom on those who would praise thee,
With Zagreus-Bacchus and Mother Persephone,
And Kalliope together with the Great Mother Goddess,
And Apollon, All-King, come now to bless us!

PROTEUS

Πρωτεύς

25: PROTEUS, FIRST

Proteus I call, keyholder of the Sea,
Nature's firstborn original imaginal decree.
You shape-change base matter into fractal complexity,
Coaxing life forward toward genetic diversity[124]
All honorable prophet, you are sought after by many,
You teach us what was, and whatever can be.
For Physis, the goddess of physical nature,
Appointed you ruler, O Primordial Changer.
Father, attend to our rites and your initiates bless,
With wealth, divine foresight, and, at last, a good death.

OCEAN GODS

What we call 'ancient Greece' is a late conflation of many, many different cultures, spread over several eco-regions and thousands of years. The gods of ancient Greece move, flow, and change as their embedding culture changes. For those of us who live inland, the dazzling array of ocean deities in the Orphic hymns may seem puzzling. However, Orphism grew up in an archipelago; the Greeks were and are a people of the sea.[125]

Okeanos and Tethys are primordial gods of elemental water. They do not properly correspond to any specific earthly bodies of water. Their children and grandchildren, including the Potamoi (Rivers), Okeanids, and Naids, are the *genii locorum* of inland bodies of water, such as rivers, pools, and springs.

Pontus and Thalassa are sometimes understood to be alternative names for Okeanos and Tethys, but they did not begin that way. Pontus began life as the Black Sea; his name has been attached to both the sea and its southern coast for millennia. Thalassa's name means, unambiguously, 'sea'. The Orphic hymns give Pontus and Okeanos each their own hymn but use the names Tethys and Thalassa interchangeably.

Nereus, most often understood as the son of Pontos and Gaia, began as the Aegean Sea, and today is a deep-sea god who rules the ocean floor. By late antiquity, he had been largely replaced with Triton. His daughters are the Nereids, ancient spirits of salt water; in modern Greek, 'nereid' means 'mermaid'. Nereus and his daughters are closely linked to the constellation Delphinus, the Great Dolphin, which lies near Sagittarius, but is not bright enough to be seen from many modern locations.

---

124 In the original Greek, this couplet says more literally 'you transform Nature into manifold shapes'.

125 Not to be confused with the so-called 'Sea Peoples' of the late Bronze Age.

Proteus is usually understood as Nereus' son. Like his father, he is a shapeshifter. In my personal practice, I understand him as a motive force behind the development of early sea life, closely associated with Cosmic Baphomet as a spirit driving evolutionary change. My translation reflects this understanding.

GAIA

Γαῖα

26: Gaia, Earth

Great Gaia, God-mother, All-Mother of humanity,
All-nourishing, flush-fruiting font of fertility.
Eldest immortal, you're yearly reborn,
As the mother of fecundity who calls to the corn;
With growing tumescence of the ripening ears,
You call forth the seasons, giving order to years.
In the pain of travail, you bring forth tree from root,
Giving birth to multihued multitudes of blossom and fruit.
Generous Grandmother, our immortal home,
Rejoicing in rain-smell, the ichor of stone,
You're the delicate smell of the graceful green shoots,
And the whirling of stars in their far cosmic routes.
Many-blest goddess of fruit and of seed,
With the kindhearted Horai, fulfill my great need.

METER THEON

Μήτηρ θεῶν

27: METER THEON, MOTHER OF GODS

Undying mother of every god ever blest,
You nourish us all from your mountainous breast.
Mistress, I call you, tearing through silence:
Come now, scepter raised, drawn by bull-slaying lions!
Your names are innumerable, as everyone knows,
For you are the font from which Kosmos flows.
You rule over all from your middle-world throne,
Great Gaia, foundation, you reign alone.
Birthgiver of the gods, and mother of humans,
You feed us with tenderness and the gentlest hands.
You rule over all rivers and every sea,
You are Hestia, bright-crowned and heavenly.
Goddess, Giver of Wealth, I call you to me,
That you grant me good gifts for humanity.
Initiation at hand, I beg you to come,
Potnia, take delight in the loud pounding drum!
Consort of Kronos, Heavenly Elder, All-tamer,
Frenzied life feeder, O Phrygian savior,
Come joyful and exulting in our adulation,
Accept our true worship, and this holy libation.

In this hymn, the goddess is extolled as the savior of Phrygia, identifying her as Ida, the Goddess Mountain of the Vale of Troy. In classical times, this was the home of Kybele, the Great Mother of the Mountain. This goddess is one 'missing link' between the neolithic enthroned goddess of Çatalhüyük and the later Greek Rhea. In this role, her key iconographic feature is the lion throne.

Little is known about Kybele, distinct from other regional Mountain goddesses, and what we do know is almost entirely filtered through the Greek point of view. Likely, she was the state god of Phrygia. Some believe she began as a deification of the great queen Kubaba.[126]

Greeks, on encountering Kybele, sometimes identified her as Gaia, sometimes as Rhea, sometimes as Demeter, and occasionally (including at Mt Ida) as Aphrodite. When Greeks colonized the region, her worship quickly spread, first to the colonizers, and then to mainland Greece. From there, she made her way to Magna Graecia. where she was well established by the 6th century BCE, and thence to Rome. In Rome, she was often called 'Magna Mater' (Great Mother) and was generally portrayed (at least among the classes whose literature survives) as an 'exotic' goddess from the 'mysterious east'.

---

126 A Sumerian queen, ca. 2500-2330 BCE.

Like many gods of the Orphic hymns, her rite appears to have been orgiastic and ecstatic, marked by drums, wine, and all-night dancing. Along with her consort Attis, she had a castrate male priesthood, about whom we know very little. For this reason, she is understood by many modern worshippers to be a special protectress of trans people. Certainly, this is in keeping with the broad family of goddesses into which she falls. The Great Mother is the mother of all people and all life, and (despite some claims to the contrary) she does not discriminate. The Great Mother of All is, in fact, a very good mother to all. She is loving, accepting, and nurturing.

The modern name of Mt Ida is Kaz Dağları, or Goose Mountain. The goose, of course, is an ancient and powerful symbol of the Great Goddess. In Greece, she was particularly associated with Aphrodite and Rhea. In Rome, geese were sacred to Juno. Today, the Lady of Mt. Ida is celebrated in a festival in late August, dedicated to Sarıkız, the 'Fair Maiden.' Local legend tells us that there was once a beautiful and good-hearted girl, who was a goose herder. After her mother died, she and her father moved to a village at the foot of the mountain. When her father went on pilgrimage, Sarıkız was left in the care of a neighbor. However, the local men took the opportunity to aggressively pursue her. She turned them all down, but the men spread malicious gossip and salacious lies about her. When he returned, her father believed those lies. He took her and her geese up to the top of the mountain, planning to sacrifice them. When there, he asked her to fetch some water, and was astonished to find it salty. He asked her to bring more water and watched her from hiding. She grew as great as a goddess and dipped the water up from the Aegean. Realizing his daughter had ascended to mystic sainthood, he was deeply ashamed, and climbed to a neighboring peak to repent and die. I do not know the origin of this legend, but it was in local circulation as early as the 14th century CE. I like to think that Sarıkız and her redemption tell of a goddess, and her sacred mountain, who can never be forgotten or thrown down, no matter how many lies are told about her.

HERMES

Ἑρμῆς

28: HERMES, GUIDE
Sara's Preferred Version:

I sing of High Hermes, belov'd worker of wonder,
First Pleiades conceived when she dreamed of bright Thunder.
All-powerful game-master, lord of the dead,
true-thinking foreteller of what lies ahead,
Code-cracking con-artist, jail-breaking the shibboleth,
killed peacock-eyed Argos when you bored him to death.
Winged-sandaled human-friend, fast philanthropic prophet,
rejoicing in racers and instructing pickpockets.
You spin hermeneutics like you're spitting hot rhymes;
You're the father of fraud, rearing up lies.
But that same trickster offers genuine peace,
Blameless, irreproachable machine of surcease.
Corycian[127] luckbringer, blessed loquacious one,
Comrade of the worker and those under the gun,
Employing clever rhetoric, venerable friend,
Pray for your initiates when our lifetimes end:
Boast about our work and our charismatic rhymes,
Memorialize our memories for future lifetimes.

28: HERMES, GUIDE
More literal version:

I call Hermes, God's envoy, the son of Queen May,
Almighty heart-bearer, Lord of the Game.
Wily wise messenger, O killer of Argos,
Winged-footed philanthropist, lover of *logos*,
Prophet of athletes, who rejoices in fraud,
Rearing up lies,[128] you're the capitalist's god.[129]
But those same hands offer genuine peace,

---

127 'From Korykos', now called Kizkalesi, on the southern coast of Turkey. In antiquity, an important mint was located there.

128 The word here, τροφιοῦχε (trofiouxe), is what's called a hapax, that is, a word that only occurs once in the classical cannon. I am reading it as 'τροφά' (rearing) and 'οὐχ', the proclitic form of οὐ, 'no, not', hence "rearing up lies".

129 The word κερδέμπορε (kerdempore) is a hard one. Liddell & Scott (the premier lexicon of classical Greek) says of it "presiding over gain in traffic". Athanasskis renders it "profiteer". I think the root words are κερδία which means something like 'greedy for gain' and ἔμπορε which means 'marketplace', like the English 'emporium'.

Blameless, irreproachable machines of surcease.
Corcian luckbringer, blessed loquacious one,
Comrade of the worker and those under the gun,
Employing clever rhetoric, the fearsome weapon of speech,
Listen to your mystics as we pray and beseech:
Give a good end to a life of good works,
Grant us memory, charisma, and eloquent words.

HERMES' LEAP OF FAITH ROAD-OPENING SPELL

This spell is designed to give a little nudge of luck that smooths the way to almost any goal.

You will need:

- copy of the Hermes ikon and a way to color it
- a magic pen
- a gold or white candle
- an oil made with sandalwood, lemongrass, and nutmeg (or any road opening oil)
- frankincense, and a way to burn it

What to do:

Whatever your goal is, you'll need to start by writing a detailed description of it. Usually, I find this easiest by writing a bulleted list of specific criteria. The more specific you can be the better. Remember, Hermes can be a bit of a trickster; be careful what you wish for. Once you have a finished list, you'll need to reduce it down to a single phrase (like 'secure a great new job'), and then to as few words as possible ('great job'). Once you have your goal all sorted out, open magical space, time, and consciousness. Light the frankincense.

Recite aloud the Orphic Hymn to Hermes, and then use your magic pen and your best penmanship to write your list on the back of the ikon. Recite the hymn a second time. Write your short goal just outside the bottom right of the ikon's bounding circle, as if Hermes were preparing to step onto it. There should be a gap between the cliff and your goal.

Next, color in the ikon, while speaking out loud to Hermes, praising him, and nicely asking for what you want. You may wish to weave sigils, seals, magic words, or symbols into your design. This should take at least half an hour. When you are done, recite the hymn one more time. Use your magic pen to write the following symbols[130] to make a bridge from the cliff to your goal.

口 ⋆ Υ ƷƷ ～ Η ✳ ᴧ. ⌣⌣ Κ Ɔ Ƈ Κ

Center into your most magical self. Anoint the candle with the oil, focusing on your goal. Speak to the candle, telling it what is happening, and expressing your wish.

Place the candle in the center of the ikon, and light it. Let it burn the whole way down.

When your wish comes true, say "Thank you" and make additional offerings.

---

130 From PGM VII 919-924, 'Hermes' Wondrous Victory Charm'. Hans Dieter Betz, *The Greek Magical Papyri in Translation, Vol. 1 Texts* (Chicago: University of Chicago Press, 1996), p. 142. 'Hermes' Wondrous Victory Charm' in *The Greek Magical Papyri in Translation, Volume 1: Texts* (Chicago: University of Chicago Press, 1996), p. 142 (PGM VII 919-924).

PERSEPHONE

Περσεφόνη

29: Persephone, Death Bringer

Persephone, daughter of Zeus the tremendous,
We beg you to bless us with the grace of your presence.
Revered only child of the great Mother of Rice,
We call out to you now: Accept our sacrifice!
Plouton's all-venerable and much honored wife,
You are the ever beloved Giver of Life.
From deep in the heart of the Earth where you dwell,
Power flows out like honey through the gates of hell.
So too, like honey, flows your lovely hair,
Praxidike, Justice Enactor, firm but fair.
Mother of the Kindly Ones,[131] underworld queen,
Holy child of Demeter, She of the Freen.
Zeus' lovechild, secretly gotten with child:
Eubouleus the shapechanger, loud-shouting and wild.
You frolic with Horai who dance forth the seasons,
Beautiful brilliance bringer, bright beyond reason.
August all-ruler, Oh radiant horned[132] one,
Pregnant maiden whose fruits ripen in sun.
Rejoicing at springtide, in the meadow's fair breeze,
Your body at one with the unfurling leaves,
You recline in a bower of ripening fruits,
But then autumn comes, and you retreat to the roots,
And come, at last, to your good marriage bed,
Salving life's pains with the peace of the dead.
Persephone, who rules from hell's shining hall,
You feed us forever, you bring death to all.
Blessed goddess who brings forth the fruits of the land,
Blossoming peace, you hold out your hand,
Granting long life and gentle good health,
bringing the blessing of a lifetime of wealth,
Easing the passage to your throne deep below,
Where you rule as high queen beside wealthy Pluto.

---

131 See hymn number 70 for the Eumenides for more on this name for the Furies.
132 'Horned' here probably means 'like the crescent moon'.

Pictured above is the deep cavern inside the Plutonion of Eleusis, the sacred cave where Persephone re-enters the world each spring. If you ever have the chance to visit Eleusis (modern Elefsina, about 20 km east of Athens) I strongly urge you to do so. My first visit there was, without compare, the most spiritually powerful experience I have ever had. The particular rock fissure above is the 'tunnel' to the underworld. However, I do not recommend journeying down this cave unless you have a lot of experience. This is a path up from the underworld; descending here means going against the natural 'flow'. Instead, call your loved ones up to you for a visit.

DIONYSUS

Διόνυσος

30: DIONYSUS, NEW GOD

EUOI!
Loud-shouting, I summon Dionysus to revel
First-born, double-formed, thrice-born devil.
Prince Bacchus, of the secret wild hidden places,
Two-horned, crowned in ivy, with two bull faces,
Martial one, reveler, holy and blest,
You feast, triennially, on human flesh.
Luxuriantly wrapped in luscious frondescence,
Laden with grapes, in form and in essence,
Zeus' child begot in unspeakable sin,
Persephone's Beloved child daemon.
Listen to my voice, with a generous heart,
Come with your nurses, fair girdled and smart,
Descend into my body with joyful quaking,
Stir up inspiration and enlightenment waking.

The name Dionysus (Διόνυσος) is difficult to provide an etymology for. Some scholars believe the name to be of non Indo-European origin, one of the lost languages indigenous to the Aegean region prior to the arrival of the Indo-Europeans. Its earliest attestation is in the 13th century BCE, where it appears in Mycenean as Di-wo-nu-so. Many, but by no means all, scholars agree that the first part of the name derives from the Indo-European dyḗws, a root which means something in the vicinity of 'sky' or 'heaven' or 'god'. It is the origin of the names Zeus and Jove, as well as English words for religious and divine matters beginning with theo- or dei-. The second part presents more trouble. Personally, I most often understand it as a version of *neos* (νέος), which means 'new' or 'young', which allows for the fun translation of Dionysus as 'Da New Zeus'.

Many understand Dionysus' name to mean 'God of (the place called) Nysa'. 'Nysa' is the name Homer gives to a place now called the Pangaian (All-Gaia) Hills in modern Macedonia, legendarily the birthplace of Dionysus. It is perhaps also perhaps related to '*Neša*', an ancient Hittite name for the place we now call Kültepe (Ash Hill), in central Turkey. There are several other potential locations; for the most part, 'Nysa' appears to be a sort of generic reference to a mysterious east, similar to the English use of 'Shangri La'. The fact that there are so many distinct ancient places called Nysa leads me to suspect that the place is named for the god, rather than vice-versa.

However, there are many other ways to read his name. One option is to tie it to *nussa* (νύσσα), which means 'post'. The word is most often used, in classical Greece, to mean a turning post at the beginning and end of each lap of a race. As it relates to Dionysus, the nussa is the post around which the world turns, the Axis Mundi. For example, the 6th century BCE mystic and intellectual Pherecydes of Syros, legendarily the teacher of Pythagoras, puts forward this position, explaining that before it meant 'post', nussa meant 'tree'. In this interpretation, Dionysus is the world tree itself. Surely 'God of the World Tree' is a fitting name for the god we also call Dendrites (Of the Trees).

More fancifully, it can be interpreted as relating to *nustazo* (νυστάζω), which means 'to nod off' or 'hang one's head' or 'drowse'. That would make Dionysis the 'God of Trance', another beautiful and appropriate name for him. Finally, I encourage you to consider 'Dionysus' as a barbarous name, to feel the shape of its vibration in your chest.

KOURETES

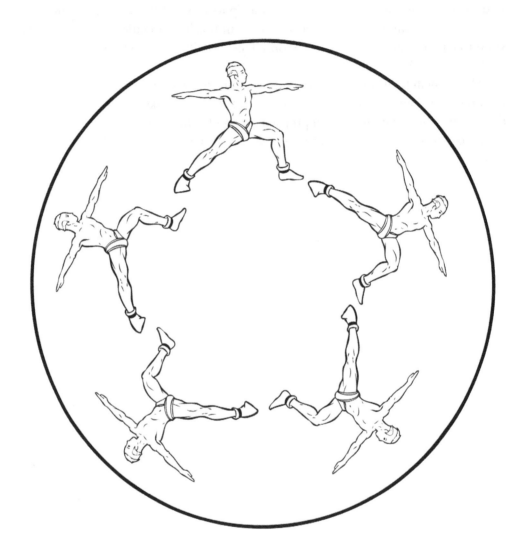

Κουρῆτες

31: KOURETES, YOUTHS

Leaping Kouretes, stomp the war-drums' thrall,
Whirl like dervishes, at the mountain bacchanal.
You bang on your lyre and dance a syncopated beat
As you leap nimble circles in your half-booted feet.
Warriors, protectors, judges splendidly famed,
Frenzied haunters of heights, wild and untamed,
Orgy-priests of the Great Mother of All,
We pray to you now, please hear our call:
Come and be gracious, with open-hearted words,
Speaking good omens for your initiate oxherds.[133]

There are two hymns to the Kouretes, this one and number 38. A group of five (or occasionally, three or nine) young daemons of Cretan Ida, the Kouretes are sometimes also called the Daktyloi, or 'fingers'. They are gods of the wild mountain, and the crafts of that mountain: shepherding, hunting, beekeeping, and iron work.

Legendarily, they were the inventors of metal armor, and taught their war dances to young men of Crete as part of the boys' coming-of-age rites. They are most famous for their role guarding the infant Zeus. In order to cover the sound of his cries, they beat upon their shields while dancing their wild dances.

---

133 The word βουκόλος literally means a cowherd, but in this context, it is an initiatory title. Similarly, we sometimes call a preacher a 'shepherd' or 'pastor' in English.

ATHENA

Αθηνη

32: ATHENA, PROTECTRESS OF ATHENS

Pallas, firstborn of the great King of the sky,[134]
You are ever strong-minded, as you make battle-cry.
Cave-dwelling goddess, of powerful name,
Ineffable, mysterious, and yet of great fame.
You bound proud up mountainous heights
but the shadowy bower is your heart's delight.
You teach the young maidens to fight passionately.
With the blade named *mania*, you smite magically.
The head of dread Gorgon rests on your Aegis
You're the mother of crafts, childless and prestigious.
You drive mad the wicked, but keep the wise healthy,
Bigender craft mother, you're exceedingly wealthy.
O shape-changing she-dragon, you invented the bridle,
Thrice born goddess, most giganticidal.
You punish inequity, and give birth to great victory,
O bright-eyed god of invention, all-benedictory,
As day turns to night, bring each thing in its season:
Grant health, wealth, and peace, O goddess of reason.

---

134 Zeus.

NIKE

Νίκη

5

33: NIKE, VICTORY

Listen, mighty Nike, we mortals' delight,
you alone free men – from the drive to fight,
From grievous strife, from wrestling with rage –
You choose the winner when wars are waged.
When battle-cries pierce through the trembling air,
you are the sweet answer to every man's prayer.
You rejoice in abundance of heroic stories,
For yours is all rivalry, all strength, and all glories.
Blessed One, we pray, come with bright shining eyes,
And bring eternal honor as nobility's prize.

NIKE'S SACRED WREATH OF VICTORY

The most potent of Nike's symbols is the laurel wreath. The plant is also closely associated with Apollo, because bay laurel grows all over Delphi. There, it was chewed by the Pythian oracle while she prophesied. Additionally, it was awarded to the winners of both athletic and poetry competitions at the Pythian Games, a practice which has spread throughout our culture.

To this day, the laurel wreath is so closely associated with Victory that it is referenced in a number of English idioms. We say that someone is 'resting on their laurels' when they are content to bask in previous successes and no longer have any ambition to create more. We also use it in phrases such as 'poet laureate' and 'baccalaureate'. Laurel wreaths are easy to buy or make, and are an excellent talisman of success. I recommend tying the laurel branches to a wire frame with red ribbons on which you have written Nike's hymn with magic marker. Talismans can also be made from small golden charms of laurel wreaths, which are particularly easy to find in graduation season.

NIKE'S WREATH OIL RECIPE

This oil, which is very similar to hoodoo-style Crown of Success oil, is easy to compound and can be used in a variety of situations. Before heading into a contest or evaluation of any kind (such as an exam or job interview), anoint your temples with the oil, and then recite the hymn to Nike while visualizing a wreath of victory being placed on your head. It can be used to anoint papers (such as applications for grants). Additionally, it can be added to oils used in lamps or used to dress a candle. For most Nike-related purposes, the candle should be gold.

The oil, when made as directed below, will keep for about three months at cool room temperature, or indefinitely in the refrigerator. The recipe is quite flexible; you can adapt it to your own use. You can also combine bay laurel and frankincense as an incense for victory magics.

You will need:

- 1 cup olive oil, the essence of the land
- 1 oz bay laurel essential oil
- 2 oz frankincense essential oil
- 9 whole bay laurel leaves
- a small magnet, to draw success to you
- gold flakes or a small gold coin, to bring wealth
- a glass bottle into which everything fits

I like to 'label' this oil by tying a laurel wreath charm onto the neck of the bottle with red silk thread.

APOLLON

Ἀπόλλων

34: APOLLON, DESTROYER

Come, blessed Paion, O bestower of bliss,
Greatly honored as Horus in the city of Memphis.
Giant-slayer, Aeolian,[135] all-shining Lykoreus,
Lyre player, you ARE the golden lyre itself.
Mouse-killer, who slew great Python in battle,
You taught us to domesticate the wild cattle.
Delphic seer, wild daemon, light-bringing marcher,
Bright beautiful and famous far-darting archer.
Leader of the Muses, joy maker, bliss bringer,
You have many names, and one might be Throat Singer,[136]
Or your Beloved bedfellow, fair Brankhos, that riddler,[137]
the all-seeing eye and oracle of Didyma?
O beautiful light-bringer with hair of bright gold,
You rule from the Cycladic center[138] of the whole world,
Your prophetic voice rings clear and true,
But I beg you to listen as I cry out to you,
For I pray for these people with passionate heart,
With true spirited words and poetical art:
From boundless aether above, you look down on the Earth,
From the darkness before every brilliant dawn's birth.
From the starry-eyed dark, in the silence of night,
You see the roots deep below and the far cosmic heights,
You are the beginning's big bang and the end of all things,
Bringing on blooms with a gentle pluck of your strings
On your many voiced kithara,[139] harmonizing the trail,
That leads lowest to highest in the Dorian scale.
You balance extremes and sustain biodiversity,[140]
Harmonizing men's fates into world-wide sociality.

---

135 The specific place referenced is the ancient city of Gryneion.

136 The Greek word Βράγχιε (Brankhos) appears nowhere else in the ancient Greek corpus. Athanassakis chooses to interpret it as a misspelling of Bacchos, but I think it is more likely associated with Bronchos (throat/lungs/brochii).

137 Like those at Delphi, oracular prophecies at Didyma were often in the form of riddles.

138 Delos.

139 A large lyre-like stringed instrument, source of the English word 'guitar'.

140 The Greek upon which these two lines are based reads "πάντα πόλον κιρνὰς κρίνεις βιοθρέμμονα φῦλα, ἁρμονίηι κεράσας τὴν παγκόσμιον ἀνδράσι μοῖραν". Literally, this is 'You balance the poles and keep the races distinct, you harmonize men's fates'.

You mix winter with summer, you equalize both,
Rumbling through winter with your lowest notes,
trilling the summer with high-noted insight,
And in spring, the season of flowering delight,
Your much-loved refrain is the Dorian mode.
O prince of we mortals, greatly honored in ode,
Called Pan, double-horned, wind whistling man,
The cause and cosmic seal adorns your right hand.
Hear, blessed savior, your initiate's voice,
Accept our olive branch and with us rejoice!

THE TALE OF FAIR BRANKHOS & THE ORACLE OF DIDYMA

The Temple of Apollo at Didyma was intended to be a twin to Artemis' temple in Ephesus; in fact, the name 'Didyma' means 'twins'. Apollo's temple there was a great wonder, and his oracle one of the most important in the Grecophone world. Legendarily the temple of Didyma, and the oracle there, were founded by the Miletan shepherd Brankhos.

Brankhos was given his name because of a vision his mother had while birthing him. She dreamed that she swallowed the sun, it grew round and hot in her belly, and finally she gave birth to a shining baby boy, whom she named Brankhos, or Throat. Brankhos never lost his shine; he grew into a golden-haired beauty. One day, as Brankhos tended his flocks, Apollo saw him and was taken with his beauty. Smitten, the god devised a plan. He hid himself in a secret meadow where he knew Brankhos would come to graze his sheep. There, Apollo laid down, and began to play sweet music. The music enchanted Brankhos, who grew more and more excited to find its source. When Brankhos finally saw the god, shining with beauty, he was overcome.

They made love, and in intimate whispers, Apollo taught him the secret wisdom, and blew the voice of prophecy into his tongue. The god crowned Brankhos with laurel, and made for him a staff of its wood. There, at the place where they shared their first kiss, Brankhos struck the ground three times and his staff grew roots and branches. Soon, he stood beneath a laurel tree, the twin of the one at Delphi. Around the sacred laurel, Brankhos built a temple to his lover, Apollo of the Kiss. There, he and all his inheritors spoke prophecy in the mysterious voice of their beloved, and interpreted those riddles for supplicants.

The earliest archaeological evidence yet found at Didyma dates it to the 8th century BCE, although classical sources thought it far more ancient. There, priestesses gave oracles at a sacred spring, interpreted by an order of priests known as the Branchidae. The temple was destroyed during the Persian invasion in 494 BCE. The Persians looted the idol of Apollo, and shortly thereafter, the spring ran dry, and oracles ceased to be told. One hundred and sixty years later, it was liberated by Alexander, who had the temple rebuilt far larger and grander. By 300 BCE, the idol had been restored to the new temple, the spring was flowing, and oracles were being told there once more.

Over time, the oracle and temple at Didyma slowly became corrupt. For example, the Roman emperor Hadrian was permitted to speak oracles in the name of the god. Like many Greek temples, the temple of Apollo at Didyma was shuttered in the late 4th century CE, and later converted into a church.

LETO

Λητώ

35: Leto, Lady

Blue-veiled Leto, holy mother of twins,
Great minded daughter of the god we call 'Questions',[141]
Heavenly Queen, much sought after in prayer,
As fate decreed it, you struggled to bear
The children of Zeus, grandchildren of Light:[142]
First, Artemis who pours arrows into the night,
Was born on Quail Island[143] off Sicily's coast,
And then Phoebos emerged on rocky Delos.
Hear us, O Goddess, O kind-hearted empress,
Come to our rites, ever pleasant, and bless us.

Leto is the goddess of prophecy by day and her sister, Asteria (who is Hekate's mother) is the goddess of prophecy by night.[144] Here is a story about them from my personal mythology:

❊ ❊ ❊

Long before Asklepios was born, the healing serpent temple of Kos was sacred to Leto the Swan Maiden, the midwife, the initiator of young woman. There, in the cave called 'White Womb of the Earth', Leto went Below. Many oaths she swore to her grandmother, Gaia, pledging herself to the Old Powers of the Earth. Among these oaths was that she would bear no children of her body. Leto went Below as a maiden, and she rose again as a goddess. Year piled on year, and century on century, and Leto began to crave children. Year piled on year, and century on century, and the pull was simply too strong. Leto forswore her vow, and ran off with the Bull of Heaven, whose hoofbeats make the thunder. The Great Mother of All was angry, and she forbid all the land to give Leto shelter on which to bear her children.

---

141 Koios is the Titanic axis mundi and the ancient pole star, Thuban, in the constellation Draco. His name is sometimes interpreted as coming from the Ionic Greek form of the interrogative word *poios*, which means 'what?', 'which?', or 'of what kind?'. He is a god of the intellect. We'll discuss him further in the commentary on the Titan's hymn (37).

142 In addition to her father Koios, Leto's mother, Phoebe, is also a Titan of Enlightenment. From her, Leto and her sister Asteria inherit the gifts of (respectively) Day and Night Prophecy. Day prophecy is then passed on to Apollo. Night prophecy is inherited by Asteria's daughter, Hekate.

143 Asteria, upon hearing of her sister's travail, flung herself into the ocean to become Ortygia, Quail Island, a place unmoored from the earth, where Leto could give birth.

144 Both astrology and oneiromancy.

Long before it belonged to Apollo and Artemis, the sacred island of Delos was Asteria's, the sister of Leto, the Lapis Queen, the goddess of prophecy by night, the initiator of young men. Asteria went to their grandmother, Gaia, and begged for the life of her sister, that she be allowed to deliver safely. Gaia refused. Asteria swore to descend herself, from the starry heavens, and become the island of quails, but even that was not enough. Finally, Asteria swore her own virgin daughter, Hekate, to the service of the Old Powers of the Earth in Leto's place. Only then was the Great Mother appeased.

So the exchange was made. Asteria fell to earth, and there, midwifed on her sister's breast, Leto was delivered of golden-haired twins. In the east, Hekate entered into the service of the Old Powers of the Earth. Below, she learned the arts Leto had forsworn: midwifery and magic, priesthood and prophecy, magic and all the herbs of healing. She learned the ways of Aconite and Asphodel, Cedar and Crocus, Fir and Date Palm, Sweet Flag and Walnut, but above all, Mugwort and Cannabis, the sacred herbs of vision.

Year piled on year, and century on century, and Artemis, the virgin huntress, began to crave a daughter. And yet, perhaps a remnant curse of her mother's broken oath, she could not conceive. The goddess of midwives could not heal herself, and her womb lay fallow and empty. Hekate, like her mother before her, interceded with Mother of All. She begged that the fertility of her womb, unwanted and unused, might be given to her cousin. In exchange, Hekate took from Artemis the gift of prophecy by day, and thus became a goddess both dark and light. Artemis conceived and bore a daughter, the inheritor of both her mothers.

ARTEMIS

Ἄρτεμις

36: ARTEMIS, GREAT BEAR

Hear me, O sovereign, fine scion of Sky,[145]
Maiden most holy, many-named ally:
Roar as a Titan[146] when you pull back your bow,
That crescent-formed torch, alight with moonglow.
Uninitiated in childbirth, ever virgin[147] remaining,
Diktynna, midwife, take away labor's paining.
Take off our bras and let down our hair,[148]
O lover of frenzy, shake off all care,
When you head for the woods, that wildest green,
Stalking your prey, ever silent, unseen.
Fleet footed night roamer, great lover of nature,
You pour out your arrows, all-gracious savior.
Famous straight-shooter, you're butch as can be,
Wild, birth-bringing, chthonic and free.
You mold boys into men and slay wild beasts,
You're wild and free with no need of priests.
In your holy oak groves and mountainous crags
You run with the deer, bringing down the king stag.
You haunt the deep wood, with your dogs at your heel,
Cydonian[149] shapechanger, O goddess ideal.
Mistress and all-queen, bringing beauty to birth,
In splendor you bring forth the fruit of the earth,
Liberator of initiates, and ally to all,
O golden-haired goddess, heed now our call:
O goddess of mountains, grant health and fair peace
Push ills off a cliff, and freeze pain in your peaks.

---

145 Zeus.

146 Although she is not usually identified as a Titan, there is no doubt that Artemis is a very early god, perhaps paleolithic. In these old forms, she is often the Great Bear, and Mistress of Beasts.

147 In this context, 'virgin' means a woman who has not born a chid.

148 The entire third line here translates the Greek λυσίζωνε. It usually means 'to unfasten a belt', but can metaphorically mean anything from unarming an opponent in battle to removing one's own armor afterwards (the opposite of 'girding one's loins'). It can also reference breaking the hymen of a virgin or dilating the cervix in preparation for birth. Similarly, it can mean to seduce (like the English 'get in their pants') or to prepare a woman for rape (similar to 'spread her legs'). In this hymn, λυσίζωνε is used as a bridge between describing Artemis as a midwife and as a frenzy-loving huntress.

149 Cydonia was an ancient city on the northwest coast of Crete, beneath modern Chania.

ARTEMIS THE GREAT BEAR

The name 'Artemis' is very old, and almost certainly not of Greek origin, although many poetic folk etymologies tell us more about how the ancients understood her name. She was *Artemes*, safe and sound, pure and intact. Others called her *Ari-Themis*, who is very like to her great aunt Themis. Personally, my preferred etymology is *Ark-temnis*, She of the Bear shrine. The most famous such bear shrine of Artemis was that at Brauron. There, in a ritual called *arkteia*, girls became initiates of Artemis. We know little of the particulars of the ritual, but it appears to have involved dancing while wearing bear skins and masks. These *arktoi*, or little bears, wore the *krokopeplos* and lived, for a time, wild, free, and pure, guarding their virginity and holding themselves apart from 'civilization'.

SELF-INITIATION INTO THE CULT OF THE GREAT BEAR

The ritual that follows is loosely based on PGM VII 686-782. It best preformed outside, under a full moon, in the Northern hemisphere, with the Great Bear visible in the sky.[150] Adapt it to suit your own needs.

You will need:

- A bear mask.
- A yellow dress or robe, ideally one that opens down the front (like a bathrobe). It will probably get stained.
- A salve of red ochre in solid fat. Bear grease is ideal, but ghee, coconut oil, shea butter, or similar are also ok.
- A substantial edible offering for the Great Bear. Fish, berries, nuts, and honey are especially nice choices. You'll eat part of it, so choose only things you and bears both like. Make the offering plentiful and enticing. If there is not sufficient offering, you may find yourself, while possessed, eating things Bear likes and you do not, such as worms or bugs.
- A blueberry, or another fruiting plant native to you, which you should plant, or commit to doing so when the season is right.
- Cool clean water in abundance. You'll drink some.
- Recorded drum sounds and a way to play them. You can't drum yourself, because you need both hands free.
- About an hour of magical space/time/consciousness.

---

150 The constellation ursa major is circumpolar; it is always in the northern sky. However, it is best to do this ritual at a place and time where the weather and light conditions permit you to see her with the naked eye.

In the weeks and days prior to the initiation, practice the invocation several times. You don't need to say it exactly word for word, but you won't be able to read from notes. By that point in the ritual, you'll be mostly Bear, and bears can't read. Come fasting, pure, and freshly washed to the ritual. Strip naked, and draw spirals, chevrons, and other paleolithic-seeming patterns on your skin with the red ochre fat. Put on your robe, trying not to smudge the drawings.

Ideally, this rite should be performed outdoors, somewhere you can be naked. If you must stay inside, that's ok. If possible, when indoors, perform the ritual in a basement or otherwise under the earth. If that is not possible, just pretend you're in a cave.

Begin the drum sounds. Put on your mask. Dance as a Bear. Dance Bear until you are sure you are mostly Bear. Look up at the moon, and say (something inspired by)...

"Bear, Bear, you who rule the heavens, the stars, and the entire world; you who make the axis rotate, you who control the whole cosmos by only force and will, I appeal to you, imploring and supplicating that you accept me into your cult and coterie; let me be your sister.[151] Bring me into the Circle Deep, the well of my most ancient ancestors.

"Do this thing because I call upon you by all your holy names, at which your divinity rejoices, which you cannot ignore: Roaring One, Earth-Breaker, Queen of the Hunt, Dildo-wearer[152]... AMOR AMOR AMOR, I E A, shooter of deer AMAM AMAR APHROU, All Queen, Wish Queen, AMAMA, well-bedded, all-seeing, night-running, man-attacker, man-subduer, man-summoner, man-conqueror, Bright One, Shining One, Ethereal One, Strong One, O lover of song and dance, protectress, spy, delight, delicate, protector, fire-bodied, light-giving, sharply armed. Admit me into your cult, accept me into the Circle Deep."

...and then go right back to dancing. Dance, feeling that this ritual (or almost this) was performed by your ancient, ancient ancestors. Tens of thousands of years of foot beats whisper around you. The ancestors are coming to join you! Dance, dance, dance, Great Bear, and feel all the others dance with you. When you cannot dance anymore, when you are a tired bear, eat half the offering, drink some water, and go to sleep to dream bearish dreams. You'll be human again when you wake.

---

151 If 'sister' doesn't feel right for you, choose any term of loving connection.

152 The epithet here is Baubo, about which you can learn more in Mise's hymn (42).

TITANS

Τιτάνες

37: TITANS, HONORED

Titans! Splendid children of Earth and Sky,
Eldermost ancestors, in Earth's womb you lie.
From the innermost nooks of the Great Below,
Timeless and ancient, you eternally flow.
Asleep deep beneath Tartarean soil,
You gave birth to all mortals who suffer and toil:
The maritime, the feathered, those of the earth,
Every life in the cosmos, you brought to birth.
I summon you now, and I beg you approach:
grant a divorce from all difficult ghosts.

The Titans are, in the simplest of terms, the gods of the Golden Age. They are primeval forces, the parents and elder siblings of the gods we all grew up with. The Titans are the *primum mobile* of Greek mythology; they set in motion the forces that shape the world. This hymn is among the only sources to support their worship as a collective. M. L. West explains this in his treatise on the *Theogony*: "There can be no certainty that they were ever worshipped: they may have existed from the beginning as 'the former gods' or 'the gods of the underworld', a mythological antithesis to the gods of the present and of the upper world."[153] And yet, it is precisely this that makes them so appealing for our modern world. Abstract, complex, and more temporal/informational than spatial/material, the Titans provide a pantheon almost ideally suited to the modern age. These are not the lusty rustic gods of an agrarian world, but neither are they the intellectual philosopher's gods of the enlightenment. The Titans are fractal where the Olympians are linear, indeterminate where the Olympians are causal. Neither immanent nor transcendent, the Titans are alien and yet extraordinarily familiar.

As we usually understand them today, the Titans are a group of twelve goddesses and gods, the children of Gaia and Ouranos, who ruled before Zeus and the Olympians came to power. Early sources disagree on their exact names and even their number, but almost all later myths hew close to Hesiod's telling in the *Theogony*. My loose translation of lines 131-138 are below:

---

153 Hesiod, *Theogony*, ed.by M. L. West (Oxford: Clarendon Press, 1966), p. 201.

From the intimate intercourse of Heaven[154] and Earth,[155]
The deep-eddying Ocean[156] was then given birth,
Next Question[157] and Brilliance,[158] the Highest[159] and the Holy[160]
The Ruler[161] and the Piercer,[162] Order[163] and Memory,[164]
And the Suckler[165] who nourishes all at her breast.
Earth bore Flow[166] and then Claw,[167] who was the youngest.
His mind was as sharp as a blade, cunning and clever,
And he hated his father, that lusty old lecher.

These twelve gods, half of whom have their own hymns in this collection, are quite unlike each other, and there is reason to believe that Hesiod was the first to group them together as siblings.

Okeanos and Tethys, similar to Apsu and Tiamat from Babylon, are primordial water divinities, from whom all life emerges. Koios and Phoebe are Light-Bringer gods of the mind, Koios the polestar of the scintillating light of reason and Phoebe the shining luminescence of wisdom. They are the grandparents of Apollo, Artemis, and Hekate. Hyperion and Theia are the primordial King and Queen of Heaven, and the parents of most of the light-bringing celestial bodies, Selene, Helios, and Eos in particular. Mnemosyne and Themis are the goddesses of Greek culture and tradition, the former the goddess of memory and the mother of the muses and the latter the law-giver and mother of the Fates. Krios and Iapetus are more obscure, keepers of the wilds and the mountains, the gods of the South and West respectively (as Koios and Hyperion are the gods of the North and East). Finally, Rhea and Kronos are the Mother and Father of the Olympians. Their stories and character are almost certainly influenced by similar myths from the East.

---

154 Ouranos, his hymn is number 4.

155 Gaia, hers is number 26.

156 Okeanos is hymn number 83.

157 Koios.

158 Phoebe.

159 Hyperion.

160 Theia.

161 Krios.

162 Iapetus.

163 Themis, hymn number 79.

164 Mnemosyne, number 77.

165 Tethys, number 22.

166 Rhea, number 14.

167 Kronos, number 13.

Some Titans are natural forces, and some are abstractions. Most are associated with the mind, and with time. Some are highly anthropomorphic, with relatively detailed stories from ancient days, whereas some were always misty and ephemeral. Some were banished to the underworld, but some still continue to live on Earth with us and in the Heavens above.

For many years, it was imagined that the stories of the Titans were remnants of an older pre-Indo-European mythos indigenous to Greece, however, by the late 20th century, that theory was almost universally out of favor with scholars. They are now generally understood to have been imported into Greece relatively late. The most widely known myth of the Titans, that of the Titanomachy, is almost unquestionably inherited from Anatolia: "...the succession of the three rulers Uranos, Kronos, Zeus, and the circumstances leading from one rule to the next have a remarkable parallel in the Hurrian saga of Anu overcome and succeeded by Kumarbi and Kumarbi in turn followed by the Storm God".[168]

Scholars disagree on the origins of the other Titans and their myths, but most agree that they are a relatively late addition to the mythology, and that the understanding of them as a set of siblings is likely an invention of Hesiod himself. M. L. West says:[169]

> The Titans, as a collectivity, the Former Gods, seem to derive from Mesopotamian mythology, coming to Greece as an organic part of the myth of the succession of rulers of the gods ... Somewhere along the way, the Titans were fitted out with individual identities ... Okeanos and Tethys come from the oriental myth, though their classification as Titans is secondary and anomalous. Kronos and Rhea play specific roles in the succession story, and must have been Titans from an early stage. Koios, Phoibe, and Themis, we must now suspect, represent a Delphic contribution to the list ... Mnemosyne may be Hesiod's own contribution: she is the mother of his Muses, and he knows of her from a Boeotian cult. Hesiod may also have added Iapetus ... Krios can again be related to Hesiod ... for he is the ... grandfather of Hekate...[170]

---

168 Friedrich Solmsen, 'The Two Near Eastern Sources of Hesiod', *Hermes*, 117.4 (1989), 413-422 <www.jstor.org/stable/4476716>.

169 M. L. West, 'Hesiod's Titans', *The Journal of Hellenic Studies*, 105 (1985), 174–175 <www.jstor.org/stable/631535>.

170 In some tellings, Hekate's father is Perses, the son of Krios. Hesiod's father immigrated from ancient Cymi (on the coast of modern Turkey, southeast of Lesbos and northeast of Chios). Their family practice included many 'eastern' gods, and was particularly centered on Hekate. This is one reason Hekate figures so prominently in the *Theogony*. In fact, there is reason to believe that Hesiod's dedication to Hekate was partially responsible for her rise to prominence in mainland Greece.

The name 'Titans' provides scant clues as to their nature. Hesiod provides a double-pronged poetic etymology, stating that Ouranos conferred the name on them as a punishment, for they had strained (*titainontas*) to perform a terrible deed, for which vengeance (*tisin*) was brought down upon them. Some scholars have proposed a link to the pre-Greek glosses *titênê* (queen) and *titax* (king).

Some scholars connect the name to the Greek *titanos* (clay or dust), which derives, most likely, from Akkadian *titu* (clay). This is because of the story of Zagreus, from the Orphic tradition. In that tale, Zeus raped Gaia-Demeter, who then bore Persephone. Zeus then seduced Persephone in the form of a serpent, and she gave birth to Dionysus-Zagreus. Zeus intended to make Zagreus the king of Heaven, but Hera incited the Titans to rise up against Zagreus. They coated themselves with white dust, then captured, dismembered, and ate the infant Zagreus. However, someone (sometimes Zeus, sometimes Athena, it depends who's telling the story) saves his heart, which is later brewed into a potion, and given to Semele, who drinks it, and becomes pregnant with the second coming of Dionysus, the god we know. To punish them, Zeus smote the Titans with his thunderbolts, and from that dust humankind was born.

Jane Ellen Harrison, an early 20th century classicist and linguist, puts forward my favorite explanation in her *Prolegomena to the Study of Greek Religion*: that the Titans and their stories are the remnants of an earlier goetic/shamanic coming-of-age initiation, in which participants were ritually killed, coated with white clay to signify death, and brought back to life. However, there is little scholarship to support this view. Walter Burkert suggests, but does not defend, what he calls a "daring hypothesis" that "The Titans bear their name of *tit*-people because eastern magicians used to fabricate clay figures—*alme tit* in Akkadian—to represent the defeated gods who were used for protective magic or as witnesses in oaths."[171]

---

171 Walter Burkert, *Babylon, Memphis, Persepolis: Eastern Contexts of Greek Culture* (Cambridge: Harvard University Press, 2004), p. 39.

KOURETES

Κουρῆτες

38: KOURETES II, YOUTHS 2

With a brazen clash, the Kouretes appear
Well armored, and wielding Ares' bronze spear.[172]
From all three worlds your rich blessings gleam:
Heavenly, chthonic, and also marine.
Life-bringing breezes, cosmic saviors fair faced
Who dwell in the shrines of blest Samothrace
Where you first brought men into magical rite,
Illuminating minds with mystic insight.
You guide and protect those on the seas,
You rule over the oceans and also the trees.
Your footfalls resound, like the drum of Earth-priests;
Your bright flashing blades frighten all fearsome beasts.
The heavens resound with your loud-shouting bleat,
Dust winds up to the sky from your ever-turning feet.
The clouds in the blue take up the tune,
And down on the earth, spring explodes into bloom.
Immortal daemons, you nourish but you also bring blight,
When humans infuriate, or fail to lead a good life,
You overturn employment and scatter possessions alike,
Making men mendicants, who hopelessly hike,[173]
Groaning and grieving, like the breeze on the seas,
Deep-eddying winds overturning deep-rooted trees.
Lofty leaves tremble like waves from on high,
They topple to earth and reverb through the sky.
Kouretes, Korybantes, youthful agents of might,
Lords of great Samothrace, Zeus' delight.
Winds ever-flowing, soul sustaining cloud-murk,
You're heavenly Gemini when you do Olympus' work,
But when you breathe well, you deliver mild and calm,
Fostering seasons, yielding fruit, and greening the balm.

There are two hymns to the Kouretes, this one and number 31. There are more notes about them with that hymn.

---

172 It is possible these lines are intended as stage direction, but I recite it when I work with the hymn.

173 Some scholars believe that there is a missing section of text between the line about causing unemployment and the part about winds overturning trees, but I have chosen to bridge them.

KORYBAS

Κορύβας

39: Korybas, Whirler

I summon the great king of the ever-flowing world,
Korybas[174] the fated, martial, terrible to behold.
Koures[175] by night, who relieves us of our fears,
Savior from illusion, Korybas, who walks the frontiers.
Shape-changer, polymorphic, double divine,
Your soul is stained red with the sin of your bloodline.
Deo, the Great Goddess, taught you to change form:
And you reimagined your body as a draconian wyrm.[176]
Hear my voice, blessed one, and banish harsh rage,
Stop visions of dread and unlock the soul's cage.

This hymn, along with numbers 31 and 38, all relate to the ancient cult of young men's warrior dance, called the 'korybas'. It was an ecstatic dance preformed in celebration of the Great Mother of the Gods. Young men danced in full armor, clashing their spears and shields, accompanied by drums, sistra, and ecstatic cries. Such dancers were called *korybantes*. In addition to their skill as warriors, initiates of *korybas* were goetic wizards,[177] who practiced charms, initiatory rites, and mysteries.[178] It is said that Orpheus was an initiate, and that he first introduced this mystery to Greece.

Both dance and dancers are legendarily[179] named after Korybas, a mythic king who was the son of Kybele.[180] Some say that Korybas is the son of Demeter and Iasion. Iasion (ἰασιώνη) is *Convolvulus arvensis*, or field bindweed. A type of flowering vine related to morning glories and High John the Conqueror plant, iasion grows in grain fields, winding widdershins up the stalks. The seeds, like morning glory seeds, contain LSA, a hallucinogen similar to LSD.

Here is how I tell the story of Korybas, which weaves together elements from the myths of Korybas, Zagreus, Osiris, Joseph bar Jakob, and John the Conqueror:

❊ ❊ ❊

---

174 Korybas is a son of Kybele; his sons are the Korybantes. Some say that Korybas is another name for Attis/Adonis.

175 Similarly, this is the singular of Kouretes.

176 Notice that, in the next hymn, Demeter's chariot will be pulled by just such dragons.

177 Γόης = goetes.

178 Diodorus Siculus, *Library of History*, 5.64.4.

179 As is often the case, historically, the myth was more likely invented to explain an already existing ritual.

180 See hymn 27, to the Mother of the Gods.

Once upon a time, long before writing came into the world, the Great Mother of the Mountain made herself a son from the seed of the King. She loved the boy, nursing him at her own breast, and called him Korybas, the Whirling Crown of the Mountain. She taught him to walk her sacred circle, and she taught him the warrior's dragon dance. She taught to him to swing the labrys. She taught him the secrets of the sacred plough, which brought forth enough grain to feed a whole people. She taught him the inner secrets as well; the incantations of the mystic, the charms of the goetic wizard, and the pharmacological witchcraft of the sacred vine, which grows among the grain.

The King died, and his sons feared their younger half-brother's claim to the throne, so they castrated him, and sold him into slavery in a savage land, flat and hot and hateful. But Korybas was half a god already, and he couldn't be kept down for long. Through cleverness and sorcery, he rose high, and soon he worked in the court of the king. There, he gained fame as a translator and an interpreter of dreams, and so eventually he became wizard-vizier to the king.

Now the king had a daughter, black and lovely, brilliant and devious. She too knew the secrets of plough and axe, of mystics, wizards, and witches. The pair soon fell in love. Korybas crafted for his love a sacred labrys of sparkling quartz and taught her the warrior's dragon dance. The princess taught Korybas another dragon dance, crafting for him a gleaming golden phallus, brought to life by both their magic. However, the pair were discovered by the king, who flew into a fury, and tried to have them killed.

Together, they stole the king's horses, and fled toward Holy Mother Mountain. The king's men gave chase, but the pair outwitted them, first turning into apple trees, then into rushing rivers, and finally into a pair of huge black dragons, who flew off joyful and triumphant, whirling and twirling in the air, circle dancing round the peak of the Mother of Mountains. There they remain, whirling and wizarding, dancing the dragon dance, waiting for their people to remember them.

DEMETER

Δημήτηρ

40: DEMETER OF ELEUSIS, GRAIN MOTHER OF ELEFSINA

Deo, All-Mother, bestower of bliss,
Daemon most holy, O many-named goddess,
Demeter the corn mother, benevolent, generous
Who suckles all mortals from your bountiful breast.
Wealth-giver, hard-worker, delighter in peace,
Grain-giving goddess who oversees seeds.
You rule over the threshing and make the fruits swell,
From the caves of Eleusis wherein you dwell.
You kindle love in our hearts and water our mouths
In anticipation of grain sprung forth from your grounds.
You invented the ox-yoke, and gave us the ploughshare,
bringing forth rich harvests in response to our prayer.
You make all things grow, and love harvest time,
O hearth-mate of Bromios, divine and sublime.
Torch bearer, Chthonia, you who bring light,
Pure, kindly, and blest, all children's delight.
Your dragon-drawn chariot tears through the skies,
And whirls round your throne with ecstatic cries.
Only child,[181] but mother of ten thousand things,[182]
you're high queen of mortals, who brings forth the spring.
Many-formed blossoming, you bloom bright with holiness,
Come, blessed one, fruit with summer's great heaviness,
Deep-laden with peace, all-grace, good-order, and delight,
Bringing wealth, health, and happiness to our mystical rite.

Demeter is the daughter of Kronos and Rhea and was often paired with her brother Poseidon. Along with her daughter, Persephone, and brother, Plouton, she reigned over the great and ancient mystery cult at Eleusis, about twenty km northwest of Athens. Demeter's name, which can be spelled Δημήτηρ (Demeter) or Δαμάτηρ (Dameter), is usually translated as Da-Mater, or Earth Mother. However, by classical times, she was no longer the Earth Mother. Instead, I think it is better to understand her modern name as Dzea-Mater (Ζειάμάτηρ), or Grain Mother. Demeter is not the goddess of plants or nature or Earth. She is the goddess of the tilth

181 Literally, the text says 'only daughter' but even that is surprising, because in 'mainstream' myth, Demeter has two sisters and three brothers (Hestia, Hera, Poseidon, Hades, and Zeus). Does this point to an earlier (pre-Indo-European) strata of myth, when Demeter ruled alone?

182 The phrase 'mother of ten thousand things' is an allusion from the first chapter of the *Tao Te Ching*. The Greek here, πολύτεκνε, means 'having many children'.

(domesticated land), and of the produce of agricultural work. To equate the two is to assume that the whole world belongs to humans, to use as we see fit. Certainly, that is an easy mistake to make in our culture.

A Spell to Reap a Good Harvest

Demeter is the goddess of agriculture; she first taught it to humans. By extension, she rules over all human activities which invest labor over a long period to produce an eventual harvest. In this context, as mistress of the harvest, she is excellent for all spell work involving the long-term growth and 'harvest' of assets. In the spell below, we work with her to sell a home or other land, but it can be easily adapted for other harvests.

To perform this spell, you will need:

- An hour, ideally during the hour of Jupiter on a Wednesday
- A yellow candle
- A small glass of clean water
- Incense, preferably of storax
- A cookie, biscuit, or other small baked good. It is best if you baked it yourself. It must be made of grain.
- A printout of the ikon of Demeter on the previous page
- A way to color the ikon and a black pen.
- An initial offering of $12, ideally in US 'Three Sisters' coins.[183] These should be distributed to twelve different homeless people within a week.
- An additional offering of a piglet[184] or $120 when the house sells.

What to do:

1. Before beginning, set some appropriate noise or music to play for about an hour, as a "timer". Personally, I like drumming.
2. Recite the hymn to Demeter of Eleusis aloud.
3. While lighting/presenting your offerings, say (something like):
   "Demeter, blessed good goddess, I present you with water, fire, incense, and the bounty of your earth. Bless my endeavor here. Faithfully, I have maintained this property for ___ years. I have kept it in good repair, and held its best interests in my heart. Now, I must collect that value and move on. Help me reap the greatest harvest possible! For your help,

183 If you are not in the States, choose 12 identical coins; the symbols are more important than the value.

184 All of my animal sacrifices are made with <https://www.heifer.org/>.

I offer you these gold coins. When the house sells, I will make further offerings in your name."

4. Using any method, design a sigil (symbol) to represent your intent. If your intent is 'quickly sell my house for a high price', then you can use the sigil at the right. If you do not know how to make sigils, you can either ask Google to teach you, or you can use written words, which are extremely potent sigils in and of themselves.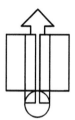

5. Carefully draw your sigil in the basket, so that the icon shows Demeter offering it to you.

6. It's ok if the entire sigil isn't visible, because some of it is 'inside the basket'.

7. Begin coloring in the ikon. Take your time and do a good job. There are no correct colors.

8. Each time you perform this spell, you may find that different colors feel right. As you color, you may want to include more sigils, words, or other magical figures in the design. Do so!

9. The ENTIRE time you are coloring, speak (or, ideally, sing) to Demeter, explaining your situation, praising her, and asking for her help. If you don't know what else to say, just repeat the Orphic Hymn (or even just her name) over and over. You may find yourself slipping into glossolalia while you color. This is EXCELLENT! Go with the flow.

10. Keep improving your ikon until your music ends. That's a signal that you may be done, not that you must be. Finish the ikon as you like.

11. When your ikon is done, kiss Demeter on the lips to activate it, and thank her.

12. Ideally, you may want to frame your ikon and display it until the house sells. Light another candle every Wednesday until the sale is complete.

METER ANTAIA

Μητήρ Άνταία

41: METER ANTAIA, MOTHER OF THE RESISTANCE

Goddess of the Resistance, mother of many shapes,
From your womb swam forth both gods and we naked apes.
You searched the world, wide-wandering, until, at the very last
You came to Eleusis, and there broke your terrible fast.
Where the dead descend, where only dust can dwell,
In the name of grand Persephone, you walked the road to hell,
for the Son of the Threshing House[185] brought you the news,
Of the goings-on in the secret bed of Chthonian Zeus.
The informant was Euboleus, the holiest Good Guide,
Whom you gave to us humans, our needs to provide.
We beg you great goddess, queen of golden grain,
Come, gracious one, sanctify your mystics again.

TRIGGER WARNING: RAPE

A ntaia (Ἀνταίη) is closely related to the prefix 'anti' in English. It means 'opposed to', 'hostile', and (some say) 'besought with prayers'. It was commonly used for Kybele, Rhea, Demeter, and other similar goddesses, both as a descriptor and an epithet. In this hymn, it clearly refers to Demeter, taking her stand against Zeus/ Hades' rape of Persephone. For this reason, I have chosen to translate it as 'of the Resistance'.

While the most common etymologies of Demeter are (as I discussed earlier) Da-Meter (Earth Mother) and Dea-Meter (Grain Mother), the Derveni papyrus provides another.[186] In discussing the rape of Rhea by Zeus to conceive Demeter, and the rape of Demeter to conceive Persephone, the author of the Derveni papyrus interprets Demeter as deriving from δέρω, which means 'to tear'. He says that is because Zeus tore her when he raped her and interprets this as an allegory of the fertile earth being torn by the rapacious plough. Here we see the shadow of the pre-agriculture indigenous peoples and ways of Greece (and the rest of Europe) falling in the wake of the conquest by Patriarchy and plough.

---

185 Dysaules, whose name means 'hard house', is the spirit of the Rharos Field, the place in Eleusis where, legendarily, grain agriculture was first practiced. His son is Eubouleus, the Good Counsellor.

186 The Derveni papyrus is the oldest surviving manuscript from Europe. It was written in 340 BCE, during the reign of Phillip II of Macedon, the father of Alexander the Great. It is a commentary on an Orphic hymn (not these exact hymns, but on of their ancestors) written in the 5th century.

Almost certainly, women in pre-agricultural Greece (and the rest of Europe) and their goddesses enjoyed more economic and political power than they retained after the transition to plough agriculture. In fact, "evidence suggests that Hunter-Gatherer societies were characterized by more independent women as compared to agricultural societies. First, it has been demonstrated that the gathering activity of women provided three quarters of the daily calorie intake of their community...the bargaining power between men and women was relatively equal in the hunter-gatherer society."[187] However, ploughs, unlike earlier agricultural technologies, require significant upper-body strength, advantaging men's work over women's, and changing the balance of economic power. "Societies characterized by plough agriculture, and the resulting gender-based division of labor, developed a cultural belief that the natural place for women is within the home".[188]

The Mother of Resistance remembers. 'Come gracious one, sanctify your mystics again.'

187 Casper Worm Hansen, Peter Jensen, and Christian Volmar Skovsgaard, 'Gender Roles And Agricultural History: The Neolithic Inheritance', *Business History eJournal*, (2012), <https://pdfs. semanticscholar.org/acac/6ede1b35492215f07824c05c01a824dc467c.pdf>.

188 Alberto Alesina, Paola Giuliano, and Nathan Nunn, 'On The Origins Of Gender Roles: Women And The Plough', *Quarterly Journal of Economics*, 128.2 (2013), <https://scholar.harvard. edu/files/nunn/files/alesina_giuliano_nunn_qje_2013.pdf>.

MISE

Μίση

42: MISE, MIXED ONE

Lawgiver who carries Dionysus' wand,
Queen Mise, sacred secret, immaculate god.
Child of the Good Guide, much-famed, many-named,
Bigender liberator, Iakkhos, breaker of chains.
You rapture in the incense of Eleusinian shrine,
And bask in the light of haloed Venus' shine.[189]
In Phrygia, you solemnize the Great Mother's rite,
And in golden grasslands[190] you grin with delight.
Your beautiful mother is Isis black-robed,
Egyptian Melanephora,[191] upon her high throne.
Nursing handmaidens tend to all of your needs,
On the banks of the Nile, thick in green reeds.
We invite you dear goddess, all well-wishing one,
Attend our mystical games and judge who has won.

Mise is one of the most obscure deities of the Orphic Hymns. There are few other references to xir.[192] In the hymn, xe is portrayed as the daughter of Eubouleus, himself an obscure figure. Xir name, Μίση, is often related the word μισέω, which means 'to hate', although there is nothing in xir hymn to explain this. Following as it does, on the heels of Mother Antaia (Mother of the Resistance), it is possible that the name indicates that Mise is the child of Demeter's wrath. However, I propose that xir name also partakes of 'μίσγω', which means 'to mix' and refers to Mise's dual-gender nature. However, the name is, originally, almost certainly of non-Greek origin. In Egyptian, *msi* means 'to give birth', and some (but not I) believe that Mise is related to the Egyptian goddess of childbirth, Meskhenet.

In the first line, xe is referred to as Thesmophoron (Θεσμοφόρον), which I have translated, as is the custom, as Law Giver. This is a cult title, very closely related to the Titaness Themis, used frequently at Eleusis in relation to both Demeter and Kore-Persephone. It could also be understood to mean 'The Carrier of that Which Has Been Laid Down' or 'Bringer of Treasure'. Thesmophoron's festival, the

---

189 In my magical circle 'shine' is slang for both the energetic glow that follows successful evocation, and also magical charisma.

190 'Grain fields' would also be accurate.

191 Black-robed Isis, or Isis in mourning, is syncretized with both Persephone and Demeter Antaia.

192 I have chosen to use a gender neutral pronoun for Mise, for reasons which will shortly be explained. I chose 'xe/xir' instead of 'they/them' because plural pronouns have specific meanings when used for deities which I didn't want to imply.

Thesmophoria, was a women-only rite held all over Greece in mid-October. The exact rites are unknown, but it is thought to have involved the sacrifice of pigs, jokes, stories, behaviors understood as 'lewd and obscene' by the mainstream patriarchal culture, and fertility magic.

In line four, Mise is also called Iakkhos (Ιακχος), usually an epithet of Dionysus. The name Iakkhos is generally understood to be the personification of the Bacchic cry ἰαχή. I think 'squeal' is a good English translation. Iakkhos (and ἰαχέω) are closely related to κοῖ (koi), which is the sound piglets make. It sounds very similar to χοῖρος (khoiros), which means 'piglet'. Bawdy puns[193] on the similarity in sound between χοῖρος (khoiros) and κυσθοσ (kusthos), a coarse word for female genitals, are common in Greek comedy.

Next, xe is referred to by titles usually associated with Aphrodite. My line "And bask in the light of haloed Venus' shine" translates ἣ Κύπρῳ τέρπῃ σὺν ἐυστεφάνῳ Κυθερείη or, literally, "in Cyprus, joyfully, you are well-crowned Kythereia". Both Cyprus and Kythira are islands classically famed for emanations of the goddess Greeks called Aphrodite Ourania, the spirit of the planet Venus.

Other than this hymn, only fragmentary references to Mise remain, so it is hard to say anything about xir with certainty. Two inscriptions to Mise were discovered at Pergamum, one at the altar of Demeter, and the other addressed to Mise Kore (Mise the Maiden). Xe is mentioned by Asklepiades of Tragilos, who says that xe was worshipped at Eleusis as the daughter of Dysaules and Baubo.[194] The 5th century dictionary of Hesychius of Alexandria[195] says that xe is associated with the Great Mother, the witnessing of oaths, and insatiable female desire. He quotes Cratinus: "Lewd (misētai) women make use of dildos."[196]

While I have chosen the gender neutral pronoun 'xe' to use in modern English, in Greek, Mise is unquestionably grammatically female. Understandings of gender, particularly of queer gender, are radically different in our culture than they were in the cultures of Mise's youth, and unlike many other deities of the hymns, xe does not have a continuous tradition of worship from which to draw. I do not think there is a word or phrase in English which can adequately capture Mise's sex or gender,[197] particularly because xe is not human, nor any other kind of biologically embodied

---

193 And also a lot of really grotesque rape culture.

194 Baubo is a mirthful demi-goddess. Sorrowfully searching for her daughter, Demeter visited Baubo's home. Baubo lifted her robes to show her genitals, where she was using or wearing a dildo, the Greek name for which is 'baubon'. What exactly they did thereafter that brought a smile to weary, sorrowful Demeter's face is left to the imagination. For this and many other reasons, Baubo is often syncretized with Isis, who also possessed a magic dildo.

195 Συναγωγὴ Πασῶν Λέξεων κατὰ Στοιχεῖον (*Alphabetical Collection of All Words*).

196 Fragment 354.

197 In my head, Mise's voice says, "It's not complicated at all. I'm a chick with a dick". When I explain that is not an acceptable phrase in polite company, xe laughs and says, "My company is not polite".

person. However, I think we can confidently understand xir, in the modern world, to function as a sex-positive, femme-leaning, queer goddess of liberation in the retinue of chthonic Dionysus and the Great Mother. Both the illustrator and I experienced profound communication from Mise, who was EXTREMELY eager for xir hymn and ikon to be published.

A FEW NOTES ON THE IKON

The lifted-robe pose in our ikon is often associated with Baubo in statuary. Mise is portrayed with breasts leaking milk, as a sign of fecundity. Xe thrusts forth the thyrsus wand of Dionysus. The bow, often tied around such wands, has just come undone, and is fluttering to the ground. In ancient Greece, men who were naked in public (such as in athletic competitions) often tied a string around the foreskin of their penises to prevent the head from becoming exposed. These ties were called *kynodesmē*, or 'dog leashes'. The exposed head of a penis was considered indecent, shown publicly only by 'slaves and barbarians'. That the bow on the thyrsus has come undone is a sign that Mise is free and unfettered by conventional notions of appropriateness.

HORAI

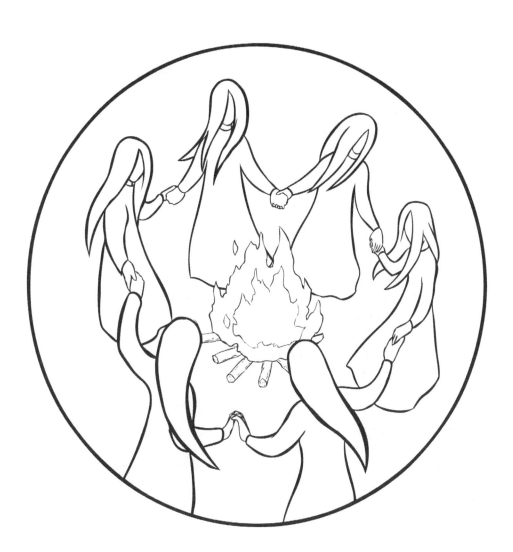

Ὧραι

43: HORAI, MOMENTS

Horai, sweet daughters of Zeus the all-king,
And Themis, (the Judge) who rules everything:
Eunomia (True Order) and Dike (the Upright),
And She of Peace, called Eirene, rich in delight.
Smell of the spring o'er the many-flowered meadow,
Pure perfumed colors wafting on wind-flow.
Evergreen Horai, in perfect circles you dance,
The bloom of the flowers in your sweet countenance.
Your dresses of blossoms are embroidered with dew,
And your playmate, Persephone, frolics with you.
You dance with the Fates and with the sweet Graces,
Until the pure pink of daybreak brightens your faces.
You're as pleasing to Zeus as all of his daughters,
And loved by the fruit-giving great Magna Mater.
Draw near to us now, as good omens you tell,
Hallow your initiates with a new mystic spell.
Give a rich harvest of fruits at their proper time,
Bless our good deeds; be kind and sublime.

The word Horai is usually translated as 'seasons', although it is also the basis for the English words 'hour' and 'year'. A more accurate translation of their name is 'intervals of time' or 'moments'. The Horai are the gods who ensure that each thing happens at its own perfect moment. In the *Iliad*, they are the keepers of Olympus' heavenly gates, determining, day by day, the proper weather.

As daughters of Themis, they are guardians of order, ruling over the proper arrangement of time. They are usually understood to be three in number, like the Greek agricultural seasons. Those three seasons are Thallo (Blooming), Auxo (Growth), and Karpo (Harvest).

In this hymn, the relevant[198] season is Spring, when Persephone returns to Earth from below, bringing the new growth with her. Persephone, the Horai, the Graces, and the Fates (half-sisters all) dance a circle together, a joyous celebration of the eternal cycles of nature.

In addition to the seasons, the Horai are also goddesses of the hours of the day. There are typically ten hours: Anatolê (sunrise), Mousikê (music and study), Gymnastikê (exercise), Nymphê (bathing), Mesembria (noon), Spondê (libations), Êletê (prayer), Aktê (food), Hesperis (evening), and Dysis (sunset).

---

198 This and some other contextual clues lead me to believe that the Orphic rite, as we have it in these hymns, was most often preformed in the Spring.

As a magical exercise, I suggest you name and sanctify your own hours. You needn't do so every day, but choose even a single day, remember it, and keep it holy. Gustave Flaubert recommends, "Be regular and orderly in your life, so that you may be violent and original in your work." Personally, life is neither regular nor orderly, nor would I want it to be, but I do try hard to sanctify each moment of it, allowing it to express its own beauty, power, and vital essence. I encourage you to do so as well.

SEMELE

Σεμέλη

44: SEMELE, BLAZING ONE

Hear me, Semele, true daughter of Thebes,
Bright beautiful maiden, regal all-queen.
Your hair, all erotic, falls over your chest,
Soon-to-be mother of twice-born Dionysus.
Then, in pain,
Glittering flame came,
And you were fiercely pierced, and fearfully seared
By Kronian Zeus' great thunder-spear.
Among all the dead, you are elevated and hallowed.
Honored by Persephone, the queen deep down below.
Your festival is celebrated in the third year,
Retelling your travail to bear Bacchus, most dear.
We sanctify your table for mystical rite
And make sacred sacrifice long into the night.
Draw near to us Goddess, come and be seen,
Your mystics beseech thee, blest Theban queen.

Semele, as we know her, is likely the syncretization of at least two currents. The first is the Thracian Earth Mother, Zemele. Little is certain about this chthonic goddess, except that one of her forms is Great Serpent. She is almost certainly related to the ancient Slavic goddess Mat Zemlya, the Mother of the Moist Earth, whose worship arose nearly 30,000 years ago on the banks of the river Don. She is an ancient, vast, and impersonal goddess, rarely given anthropomorphic form. To contact her, dig a hole in the earth and speak into it; prophecy can be sought from her in this way.[199] Her worship persisted in isolated villages until the early 20th century, and some of her rites continue still, although they are ostensibly dedicated to Mary Theotokos.

The second current is that of Semele of Boeotia, the youngest daughter of Cadmus and Harmonia who, as legend goes, lived around 2000 BCE. Semele was a priestess of the Bull of Heaven, and one day, after slaughtering a bull in his honor, went to the river to wash herself of the blood. She was seen by Zeus, whose lust was aroused. The pair fell in love and met many times in secret. When Semele became pregnant, she attracted the ire of Hera, who came to her in the guise of an old woman. Hera convinced the young woman that she had been duped. Her lover was not Zeus, but only some fuckboi leading her on with nonsensical claims.[200] She convinced Semele that she must ask 'Zeus' to prove himself by showing her his true form.

---

199 This works for most chthonic gods.

200 To be fair, this is how I would react if a guy told me he was Zeus.

And so Semele went to Zeus, and demanded that he grant her a wish. He readily agreed. She demanded, as Hera had instructed, that he reveal himself in all his divine glory. He quailed, knowing no mortal could survive such a vision, but she held him to his oath. He made himself ready, choosing his dullest robes and his most pitiful thunderbolts. He chose a most inauspicious time, when his power was least. And yet, the moment he threw off his human form, and appeared in all his glory, Semele sizzled and burst into flame. Heartbroken Zeus could not save her, but rescued the fetus from the flames, and implanted it in his own genitals (some say 'thigh'). The babe came to birth as the great god Dionysus.

Meanwhile, Semele descended into the Underworld, where she quickly became a favorite of her son's other mother, Persephone.[201] Thus elevated to heroism, it was a small matter for her to ascend to Olympus, aided by her son. There, she took the name Thyone, which means 'raging ecstasy', and became the leader of maenads.

---

201 Who bore Dionysus in his previous incarnation as Zagreus. When Zagreus was murdered by Titans, Zeus salvaged his heart, and swallowed it, thus imbuing his seed with the essence of the slain god, with which he impregnated Semele. In other versions, he brews it into a potion and Semele is impregnated when she drinks it. The prefigures the immanence of Dionysus in wine and highlights Semele's role as ur-bacchant.

BASSAREUS

Βασσαρεύς

45: Dionysus Bassareus Triennial, of the Fox Skin

Come, blest Dionysus, fire-born and bull-faced,
Come all-master Bacchus, whose name's oft replaced,
Come Bassareos, the Fox-Formed, wearing red skins,
Delighting in swords and in bloody maenads.
You're inflexible in war, and wrathful and vicious,
You cry EUOI! as you rage through Olympus.
O frenzied one! O Bacchus, shout thundering loud!
Raving and wild, storming black war cloud.
You wield your thyrsus in battle like a bronze-blazing spear,
Among all three worlds, you are highly revered.
Both gods and men praise you, and those down below,
Come leaping, blessed one, and seeds of joy sow!

A 'bassaris' is a ritual costume or cloak made of fox skin. The word, as well as the costume and custom, are probably imported into Greek from Thrace. A 'bassara' is a ritual dancer thus attired. From Hesychius' sixth century dictionary, we know that a dance called *alopeks* (ἀλώπηξ), which means 'fox', was known to him, but we do not know much more about it. Most likely, these are two names for the same dance/ritual – alopos the Greek and bassara imported, likely from Thrace. The fox-clad dancers may have been among the highest ranked Bacchic initiates. For example, in a second century CE inscription from ancient Tusculum (near Rome), there is a list of imitates and their degrees; both male and female 'Chief Foxes' are listed.[202]

Several images of such dancers have been discovered across the Grecophone world, some very ancient. At the temple of Despoina (a Mistress of Beasts closely related to Persephone) at Lycosura, a marble carving depicts female dancers in animal masks, including at least one who appears to be dancing fox.[203] Terra cotta figurines depicting people wearing fox masks have also been found at early Iron Age sites in Cyprus.[204]

Animal dances are among the very oldest and most universal types of ritual, known in every culture, every land, and every age. Almost certainly, this practice of masked/costumed dancers, ecstatically possessed by their animal spirits, is the origin of the myth that the bard-magician Orpheus could make even animals dance. It may also be the ritual at the root of the Witch Queen Circe's legendary ability to turn men into beasts.

---

202 Achille Vogliano, 'La Grande iscrizione bacchica del Metropolitan Museum', *American Journal of Archaeology*, 37.2 (1933), <https://doi.org/10.2307/498439>.

203 Lillian B. Lawler, 'Two Notes on the Greek Dance', *The American Journal of Philology*, 69.1 (1948), 87–91 <https://doi.org/10.2307/291323>.

204 Lawler 87-91.

LIKNITES

λικνίτης

46: DIONYSUS LIKNITES, OF THE WINNOWING FAN CRADLE

Dionysus of the cradle: we cry out to you! Hear!
Bacchus of Nysa,[205] we beg you appear.
Ever blooming, much Beloved, all-gracious one,
Fosterling of nymphs, who loll in the sun,
And Aphrodite, the clever, the wise, and the fair,
With a bright crown of gold bedecking her hair.
With passionate fire, you dance midst the oaks,
Maenads abounding with the nymphs you invoke.
Zeus sent you away to live with Persephone,
And the illustrious mother dandled you on her knee.
She raised you beloved of the immortal ones,
Receive now your sacrifice. Blessed one, Come!

A *liknon* (λίκνον) is a type of basket used both in the winnowing of grain and as a cradle. It appears in the first line of this hymn, where I have chosen to translate it as 'cradle'. In addition to Dionysus, ancient Greek art depicts many babes, both human and immortal, sleeping in winnowing fans. While I cannot confirm this, I expect it would be very easy to rock a baby to sleep in a liknon by gently nudging it with your foot. Because both winnowing grain and rocking sleeping babes were traditionally 'women's work', knowledge about them and their sacred rites has not been well preserved. We may never know their full story.

To use such a basket to winnow, threshed grain is tossed into windy air. The light chaff (seed casings) blows away, and the heavier grain falls back into the basket. Then, a second round of cleaning is performed by shaking the basket until the lighter chaff falls out the open end. Similar winnowing baskets exist in almost all grain-agricultural cultures, in a variety of related shallow shapes, all of which are designed to arc the grain upwards when tossed. I suspect, but cannot confirm, that the basket in which Moses floated down the river was understood, by the stories' intended audience, to be a winnowing fan of some type.

---

205 See hymn number 30 for more on Nysa.

In addition to being the cradle of baby Dionysus, these baskets were (unsurprisingly) sacred to Demeter, the Grain Mother. At Eleusis, and many other sites sacred to her, the winnowing fan was revered as a sacred object. Several small clay votives in the shape of winnowing fans have been found, usually full of (clay) cakes, fruits, and other offerings. The dual association of grain and babies suggests that the liknon was likely seen as a symbol of fertility, of both field and womb. This is held out by archaeological finds at Acrocorinth, where winnowing baskets were found in conjunction with clay phalluses.[206]

---

206 Allaire Brumfield, 'Cakes in the Liknon: Votives from the Sanctuary of Demeter and Kore on Acrocorinth', *Hesperia: The Journal of the American School of Classical Studies at Athens*, 66.1 (1997), 147–72 <https://doi.org/10.2307/148477>.

PERIKIONIOS

Περικιόνιος

47: BAKKHOS PERIKIONIOS, SHOUTER OF THE TWINED VINES

I call out to you, Bacchus, wound round with the vine,
O blessed one who gave us the gift of fine wine.
In the house of Kadmos, the Theban ur-king,
Your vines coil like snakes around everything.
You calm the earthquake with your mighty hand,
When the thunderbolt's blaze rumbles the land,
When the hurricane whistles and we are set free:
We beg, bless our Bacchanal with heartfelt glee.

SABAZIOS

Σαβάζιο

48: Sabazios, Destroyer

Listen to your daughter[207] as she sings forth your ode,
Forefather Sabazios, glorious daimon of old.
Father of Eiraphiotes,[208] and the son of cruel Kronos,
You 'stitched up your thigh' bringing forth Dionysus,
When you came to the rites of the most holy peak,[209]
And took your place beside Hipta, of beautiful cheek.
Adored king of Phrygia, blessed guardian of all,
Be gracious to your initiates when we come to call.

Eiraphiotes is usually an epithet of Dionysus, of contested etymology. One folk etymology comes from εριφοσ, which means 'young goat'. However, a second derivation of the name is from ῥάφις (to stitch), and that word play was probably intended here. In addition to referencing Dionysus being 'sewn into' his father's 'thigh', this may also reference early techniques for brewing mead, by sewing honeyed water inside a skin bag.

In some other literature of the ancient Mediterranean (including Torah), 'thigh' is a euphemism for male genitals, and I believe that is implied in this story as well. What can it mean to say that Sabazios performed surgery on his genitals at Tmolos?

At Mt. Tmolos, and many other holy mountains in Lydia, Kybele (the great Mother of Mountains) was worshipped under the name Hipta, whom you will meet in the next hymn. One consecration ritual of a priest of Kybele is self-castration during ecstatic (often called Bacchic) frenzy. Does this hymn imply that the Zeus-Sabazios castrated himself in divine ecstasy, in devotion to the Great Goddess, and arose reborn as Dionysus-Sabazios?

Sabazios began life as a Thracian horse god, although his cult spread first throughout Lydia and Greece, and eventually through the Roman Empire, where he was primarily syncretized with Jupiter, but also Dionysus and occasionally Helios. In the later days of the Roman empire, there were those (including Plutarch) who syncretized him with Adonai Tzavaot, the Lord of Hosts.

Because most of the sources we have on his cult are actively hostile to it, it's difficult to know much about him. Like Dionysus, he was closely associated with intoxication.

---

207 If you prefer it, 'Hear now your worshipper as I sing forth your ode' will maintain the meter. As we've now discussed several times, the Orphic hymns are essentially an oral, rather than written, tradition. They SHOULD be different for different people.

208 Εἰραφιώτης (Eiraphiotes) is an epithet of Dionysis discussed further on page 105.

209 Mt. Tmolos is now called Mt. Bozdağ. It is in Izmir, Turkey. It is named (in Greek) after Tmolos, the oak-clad mountain king, and son of Ares. He was the first husband of Omphale who later became the dominatrix of Heracles.

His particular intoxicant of choice was probably a kind of Illyrian (Balkan) beer called 'sabaia'. Doubtless this played an important part in his cult practice. All ancient sources on the cult of Sabazios compare it directly to the Mysteries of Dionysus, to which the Orphic Mysteries are closely related. These cults were open to everyone but were associated with classes on the periphery of classical Greek culture: women, slaves, and foreigners.

At their heart, the Mysteries promise liberation, and among their core magical practices is spirit possession. The mystic becomes the horse which the god rides. Several methods of trance induction were undoubtedly used. In addition to wine, beer and mead, herbs and possibly mushrooms, as well as drums, bullroarers, and ecstatic dance may all have played important roles.

Sabazios is closely associated with an unusual cult object, called a 'hand of Sabazios'. Archaeologists have discovered such bronze right hands, raised in a blessing gesture. They appear to have been attached to the top of a staff or scepter. The hands are covered in symbols, usually including a pinecone on the thumb and serpents wound around the wrist. Various other symbols appear on different hands, including the thyrsus and many types of animals.

HIPTA

Ἴπτα

49: HIPTA, GREAT MARE

Hipta, glad maiden who took Bacchus to breast,
You shine with fierce joy when you're dancing, possessed,
Around the roaring bonfire of Iacchos' rite
Crying out 'Euoi!' to incandescent night.
While you initiate mystics into Sabazian glory
Chthonic queen mother, listen to our story:
From Phrygian Mt. Ida, Oh Goddess, please come!
From Mt. Tmolos of Lydia, we beg you, please come!
Come, your face shining with joy, suffuse with bright light,
And accept sacrifice at your mystic initiates' rite.

Hippa, or Hipta, is a very obscure goddess. Her name likely derives from that of the Hurrian Great Mother, called Hebat, Khepat, or Hepat. However, to Greek speakers, her name echoes *hippos*, the Greek word for 'horse', an important form of the Great Mother, and so she was often understood as Mother Mare. Some say Hepat is the deification of Kubaba, whom we also discussed in the chapter on Meter Theon. Kubaba is only woman on the Sumerian King List, which says she ruled for 100 years, somewhere in the early-middle of the third millennium BCE. The king list further says that, before becoming ruler, she was a brewer and tavern-keeper.[210]

Aside from the Orphic hymn, few mentions of Hipta exist save for a few inscriptions found near Mt. Tmolos in Lydia. In those, she is often paired with Sabazios-Zeus, and always called Mother. In Orphic mythology, Hipta is a foster mother of Dionysus. After being born from Zeus' thigh, baby Dionysus was placed in a winnowing basket with a snake wound around it. Hipta then carried him to Tmolos, where he was raised as a fosterling of the Great Mother Kybele. Whether Hipta is a goddess in the court of Kybele, or an avatar of the Great Mother herself is not clear.

---

210 A well-respected ancient profession often mythologically allied with witches.

LYSIOS LENAIOS

Λυσιος Ληναιος

50: Lysios Lenaios, Liberator of the Wine Press

Two-mothered Bacchus, of the sacred wine-press,
Much-recalled child of Zeus, ever blest.
Many-named redeemer, mysterious child,
Blessed daimon, EUOI! Bacchic and wild!
Happy and fat, you make the fruit grow,
Bursting forth from the earth deep down below,
Eager for the wine press and bringing delight,
Shape-changing grape angel, overflowing with might,
You ease human toil and teach us to heal,
You free us from pain, O blossom ideal!
Your beautiful hair flows down in thick waves,
Your mystics all cry: 'Come and join in our raves!'
Kindly and well-wishing, we beg you appear,
To the gods and good mortals who have gathered here.
Liberator, thyrsus-raver, loud-shouting squeal,
EUOI![211] EUOI! EUOI! EUOI!
Glad giver of fruit, bestower of delight,
Your mystics beg you attend our Bacchanal rite.

---

211 The Bacchic cry 'euoi' (εὐοî) is a sound, and not really a word. It sounds like a pig call. It is related to Dionysus' epithet Εὔιος, which means 'good boy'. Everyone says it differently, but in this poem, it's intended to have a long *eeeee* at the end.

NYMPHS

Νύμφαι

51: NYMPHS, BRIDES OF THE WILDS

The great heart of the ocean gave you Nymphs birth,
And so you dwell in wet places: holy holes of the Earth.
Bacchic, chthonic, spirits who inspire the hollows,
Who rejoice in the voice of the deep sacred grottos,
Unseen phenomena who wander the air,
Nymphs of the groves, flowering fair,
You emerge from your springs, clad only in dew,
Leaving wet, nimble footprints trailing behind you.
You ripen the fruits of the wide verdant veldt,
As you dance oblique orbits 'round the sentient umwelt.
Bacchic revelers of the hills, you dance, wanton, with Pan,
You wear only moonlight as you waltz with abandon.
You love comely goatherds in the soft moss of the oak groves,
You bear wild beasts, promoting rich growth of the droves.
O Nysian medicinals,[212] who blossom in spring,
O hamadryad maidens, mad like gadfly-sting,
Come with Bacchus and Deo,
and for the sake of mortals bring:

The liberation of the mind,
The good omens of the shrine,
Hygieia's ever pouring wine,

And the bursting forth of growth in the warmth of the spring.

Many kinds of nature spirits were called nymphs in ancient Greece. In particular, they were seen as guardians and enlivening spirits of springs and their worship in such places is very well documented, dating to well before the 4th century BCE, and lasting into the common era.

Just as Demeter gives grain, Pan provides milk,[213] and Dionysus provides wine, the Nymphs provide water. For those of you who, like me, live in places where natural fresh water is abundant, it is perhaps difficult to imagine the sacred importance of springs in more arid climates. Water is life, and it is in the Nymphs' keeping to give or withhold it. Those places where it bubbles forth in abundance are sacred places and mystical portals of great liminal power.

---

212 Healing herbs.

213 In ancient Greece, goats and not cows were the cornerstone of dairy production.

In addition to their role as providers of fresh water, the nymphs provided more mystical quenching. In humans, their power bubbles up as magical eloquence, a type of mild trance possession called 'nympholepsy', which literally means 'seized by nymphs'. In the *Phaedrus*,[214] the famed wise man Socrates, by the banks of a stream, begins to wax rhapsodic about love, and then interrupts himself, asking his companion if he seems to be possessed. The friend replies that he does seem to be speaking with "an unusual fluency". Socrates bids the man to listen attentively, warning him that "this place seems filled with a holy spirit; so do not be surprised if I, as often happens, seem to be manic as my speech continues, for I am already almost uttering dithyrambics".[215]

Note that Socrates believes the **place** itself to be the source of inspiration, a claim he repeats later.[216] "...I shall surely be possessed of the nymphs to whom you purposely exposed me...I shall cross this stream and go away before you put some further compulsion upon me."

Nympholepts delivered not just impassioned sermons, such as Socrates', but also prophetic utterance, and sacred poetry. In this, their gift is very similar to that of the Muses. The *Theogony* begins with a description of the Muses as nymphs of the Hippocrene,[217] a sacred spring on the slopes of Mt. Helicon whose waters legendarily grant the voice of True Poetry.

I have loosely translated lines 1-10 below:

With the Heliconian[218] Muses we open our singing:
Dancing a helix[219] with no end or beginning.
Dwelling on Helicon, the great holy mountain,

---

214 Plato, 'Phaedrus' in *Plato in Twelve Volumes*, 1, trans. by Harold North Fowler (Cambridge: Harvard University Press, 1914), 238c-d.

215 A type of wild free verse associated with prophecy and divine utterance in classical Greece.

216 Plato, *Phaedrus, Plato in Twelve Volumes*, Vol. 9, trans. by Harold N. Fowler (Cambridge, MA: Harvard University Press; London, William Heinemann Ltd. 1925) pp. 241e - 242a.

217 The 'Spring of the Horses' was so called because it was mythically created by the stomping hoof of Pegasus.

218 Mount Helicon (Ἑλικών) is in Boeticia, about six miles north of the Gulf of Corinth. The name Ἑλικών is closely related to the word ἕλιξ, which is the cognate of the English 'helix'. In English, we would say that Helicon is 'the helical mountain'. Unlike many sacred places described in the Orphic Hymns, which can sometimes be a bit misty with metaphor; here Mount Helicon is rendered with the intimate but clear-eyed love of a native son. Hesiod spent most of his life in the so-called Valley of the Muses, nestled in the foothills of Helicon.

219 The original text does not specify that it is a circular or spiraling dance, which would have been understood implicitly by the intended audience. To the ancient Greek, whenever groups of goddesses, like the Muses of Graces, are dancing, the implication is that they are dancing a circle dance. Thus, we have an obvious poetic etymology: Mount Helicon is the mountain of the helical dance.

Stepping delicate grace round violet[220] fountain,
Toward the bimah,[221] the high place, of Kronian Zeus'.
At the bank of the stream, pause dancing Muses,
To wash your delicate skin in Permessos' courses,
at the holy river Olmeios[222] at the Spring of the Horses,
Your feet flowing forth to Helicon's pinnacle,
The dance of creation: eternal and cyclical.
Rise from high peaks, clothed in delicate mist-blurs
Soothsaying, night wandering, speaking beautiful whispers.[223]

---

220 The word tells us that the water in the spring is especially dark; it implies a deep well where our world and the underworld are very close.

221 The word βῆμα used here commonly means a 'raised platform' such as an orator's podium. That same word is still in use today in English as 'bimah', the dais at the front of a synagogue which houses both the ark (in which the holy scrolls are kept) and the podium from which the rabbi speaks. Both of those uses call back to the even more ancient way it is used here, to describe an altar at the highest place on a piece of land. Such altars, called במה (bamah) in Hebrew, are referenced several times in the Torah, and appear to have been ubiquitous in the greater Levant.

222 Although no one is entirely confident exactly how this ancient geography matches up to the modern landscape, most believe that the Permessos and Olmeios joined to empty into Lake Kopaida, which was drained in the 19th century.

223 Hesiod, *Theogony*.

TRIETERIKOS

Τριετηρικός

52: Trieterikos, Dionysus of the Triennial Festival

I summon you, blest one, of uncountable names,
Frenzied Bacchus, the bull-headed, born from the flames,
Nysios (of the mountain),[224] Lenaeus[225] (of the wine-press),
Thigh-born liberator who delivers the oppressed.
Liknites[226] (of the cradle) who bears high the light
Of the torches that guide our procession by night.
Mystery-initiator, Eubouleus, teacher of truth,
Triple-formed love-child of almighty Zeus.
Orgiastic secret, Erikapaios,[227] primeval first born,
The father of the gods and the divine only son,
You feast on raw flesh and bear a great rod,
You delight in our dancing, O joyful god!
O Bakkhos of the blessed triennial rite,
Who grants calm quiet in the still of the night,
You burst forth from the earth, blazing with fire,
Haunting the mountains in fawn-skin attire.
You wear a fine turban, grape-bedecked horned one,
You lead annual festivals, holy two-mothered son.
You have many nurses, O babe at the breast,
You burst with great strength, eternally blest,
Bassarus, Great Fox, crowned all in ivy,
Surrounded by maidens, delightful and lively.
Battle-ready Paean who wields a great spear,
Your mystics call out: O blest one, appear!

In Greek, 'triennial' means 'in the third year'; a triennial festival is one which occurs in year 1 and again in year 3. In English, we would say such a festival occurs 'every other year', and call it 'biennial'. Many plants, in certain habitats and weather conditions, have a biennial life cycle. Their seed, slumbering in the Earth, is given birth with the spring by Persephone, then sleeps again the next winter. In their second spring, such plants awaken and blossom, and set seed to the next generation.

Immortal Dionysus is evergreen, but he also a dying and rising god. In Orphism, Dionysus is twice born. He is Zagreus, the child of Persephone by Snake Zeus. When,

---

224 The mountain in question is the Pangaion Hills of Nysa, which we discussed in hymn 30's commentary.

225 See hymn 50.

226 See hymn 46.

227 We discussed this epithet with Protogonos' hymn, number 6.

as a child, Zagreus is killed by the Titans, his essence is fed to Heavenly Zeus, by whom it impregnates Semele with the second coming of Zagreus, whom we call Dionysus. This Dionysus is himself like the biennial plants: born, die back, born again, and finally coming to blossom.

Many of the plants associated with the Orphic Rite can be biennial in Mediterranean climates. For example, it is likely that the sacred torches were made from biennial mullein. We know for sure that mullein torches were used in similar Roman processions. Mulleins are large plants with huge fuzzy grey-green leaves. When they blossom, they produce huge stalks topped with bright yellow flowers, often up to eight feet tall. When dried, these stalks can be dipped in tallow or wax to create torches. From this use, mullein derives many delightful common English names: 'witch's candle', 'fairy torch', and 'hag's taper' are my favorites.

Mullein is an excellent spirit ally, and one I suggest you cultivate if your climate allows mullein to grow. It can often be wildcrafted from roadside ditches, abandoned lots, and construction sites. It is extremely easy to grow from seed. If planted, it can be difficult to eliminate, although rarely invasive. Its smoke, in additional to being healing for the lungs, is an excellent aid to the spirit site. If you develop a relationship with Mullein, carry her stalks as torches and call on her in the Other Place to light your way.

AMPHIETUS

Ἀμφιέτᾱς

53: DIONYSUS OF THE ANNUAL FESTIVAL

Yearly we call you, O Bacchus, Dionysus below,
'midst marvelous maidens and nymphs all aglow,
Long have you slept in Persephone's bower,
Deep in the underworld, like the seed of a flower.[228]
For you sleep on the triennial cycle unending,
Sleeping below, and then upward ascending
To sing hymns with your nurses, lovely and fair,
Dressed in bright colors, with free-flowing hair,[229]
your lullaby gentles the seasons to sleep,
Then wakes them again from the earth's inner deep.
Blessed one, who ripens the greens of the earth,
Bacchus, the Horned One, who brings fruit to birth,
Come now, we plea, to our pantheon rite,
Turn your face toward us, smiling bright,
Bringing forth fruit, luscious and ripe,
Unblemished and perfect, fit for sacrifice.

---

228 'Like the seed of a flower' does not occur in the Greek, but it is implied in the reference to sleeping with Persephone, who winters, with the seeds, in the underworld, and then pushes them to bloom in the spring.

229 This entire line translates the Greek word εὔζωνοι, 'well- girdled'.

SILENUS, SATYRS & BACCHAE

Σειληνός, Σάτυροι & Βάκχαι

54: Silenus, the Satyrs, and the Bacchae

On this holy triennial festival night,
Gods and mortals together make the great rite!
We call out to Silenus, foster-father of Bacchus,
Best of the silenoi, favored by the Great Goddess.
O majestic band-leader, and founder of our orders,
You first taught bacchanal to your all-blessed daughters.
We rave with the wet-nurses, wakeful and lively,
With Naiads and Bacchants, crowned in green ivy.
With Satyrs and Beast Men performing great rite,
We howl out for the prince of bacchanal night!
You bacchante of the festival of pressing the wine,
You're all done with work; come make the night shine!
Howl out, thyrsus lovers, feel the innermost tightening,
Orgiastic initiates, feel the bacchanal heightening,
And then the quiescent calm of the sacred enlightening.

Silenus is often described as the tutor or caretaker of Dionysus; I understand him to be a foster father to the young god. His name means 'wobbly (with) wine'; he is the drunken prophet of these hymns, and among his special domains are creativity, nurturance, ecstasy, wisdom, joy, art, and mystery. In this hymn, we are encouraged to find that same state of radically open intimacy within ourselves.

In addition, he is the leader of the *silenoi* and satyrs, beast-men who dance revel for Dionysus. These are the male counterparts of the nymphs; nature spirits of the free wild places. Often portrayed as half horse or half goat, they are always lusty. They are sometimes portrayed as violent, rapacious buffoons by 'proper' ancient writers, but there is nothing here to suggest such a thing. Here, they are wise fools and puckish punks, who have given themselves over fully to divine ecstasy.

There is good reason to believe that the Satyrs began their life as the Satrae (Σάτραι), the only Thracian tribe never conquered by classical Greece. The homeland of the Satrae were the Pangaion Hills, the hills of All-Gaia. Despite the name, this is a high mountain range in northern Greece. Homer called this region 'Nysa', as we discussed in the commentary to hymn number 30.

Of the Satrae, Herodotus tells that, in his time,[230] "...they dwell on high mountains covered with woods of all kinds and snow-clad, and they are keenly warlike. They are the people that possess an oracle shrine of Dionysus and this oracle is on the

---

230 The mid 5th century BCE.

topmost range of their mountains".[231] Herodotus was shocked by their free and wild ways, writing "over their maidens they do not keep watch, but allow them to have commerce[232] with whatever men they please". Scandalous!

This hymn is one of my favorites. In many ways, it is the energetic peak of the rite. As doubtless you noticed, it is the last in a long series of Dionysus hymns. I often declaim it at the beginning of a party, and during COVID-times, when so many pagan events moved online, I often used it to help create a tiny piece of that festival atmosphere during Zoom conferences.

---

231 Herodotus, *The Histories*: vii 110 in *Herodotus*, trans. by A. D. Godley (Cambridge: Harvard University Press, 1920).

232 Sex.

APHRODITE

Αφροδιτη

55: APHRODITE, SEAFOAM ASTARTE

Aphrodite, Ourania, ever sought after,
Seaborn mother goddess, bright lover of laughter,
You delight through the night in revels and raves,
Rousing lovers to couple like you rose from the waves:
Glistening wet wile-weaver, mother of need,
All that awakens begins as your seed.
Genetrix of the universe, eternal all-queen,
You rule over all worlds, those seen and unseen –
The bright shining heavens, and the ever fruitful earth,
And the depths of the seas –
to all you gave birth.
You sit beside Bacchus, loud-shouting god of wine,
You rejoice in abundance, cheer, and good times.
You yoke people together, lover to lover,
Bringing forth love's variety, Erotes' mother.
Seductress, joy-bringer, kind-hearted Persuasion,
You coax forth our pleasures hidden within,
And lead us by hand to our lovers' beds,
where you whisper sweet nothings in our anxious heads.
With everyone watching, or in deep-secret tryst
Your hair all disheveled, your lips all raw-kissed,
You are empress and goddess, bearing queen's rods.
Honored guest at the weddings of all of the gods.
Your philters fill us with lust-frenzied greed
Locking lovers together in unquenchable need.
Desirable one, she-wolf, bringing longing and heirs,
O life-giver, love-gifter, attend to our prayers:
Come, daughter of Cyprus, and lend us your charms,
For all living creatures get lost in your arms.
We behold you, great goddess, splendid of countenance,
Whether lounging in heaven, or on high Olympus,
Or on Syrian throne, redolent of frankincense,
Richly adorned or unveiled of pretense,
Or roaming around in your iridescent chariot,
Or flanked by your priests on the river of Egypt,
Or in your swan-driven carriage upon the wide sea,
Delighting sea-creatures as they dance in your breeze.
You bring joy to the nymphs of the earth and the forest,
And those who leap lightly in sea-foamy chorus.

You are seated in Cyprus, O Queen most divine,
where your blessings are spoken by maidens most fine.
They sing for you, blest one, and immortal Adonis-
He the grain god, and you the great goddess.
We summon you now with fine words and pure souls
Hear our words, drink our wine, and smoke of our bowls.[233]

APHRODITE'S PIGEON POST

In our culture, we often think of Aphrodite as the goddess of romantic and sexual love, but she is so much more. Aphrodite is every bond that ties us human to human, weaving communities together; she is the love of parent for child, and the love of neighbor for neighbor, as well as the love that turns lovers into beloveds. Her dove is the line of communication that keeps those intimacies alive. These messengers of Venus played an extremely important role in keeping the peace among the many fractious polities that we call ancient Greece. The association of doves with the planet Venus is very old. The Greek name for them is περιστερά (peristera), which possibly derives from the Semitic 'perah Ishtar', or 'flowering of Venus'. As in many languages, Greek does not distinguish between differing species of Columbidae, using the same word for both pigeons and doves. As early as 3000 BCE, wild rock doves had been domesticated for use as messenger pigeons. They have an exceptional sense of navigation; when lost, they can always find home.

My favorite way to use this ikon magically is to send messages of the heart. Sometimes, for a variety of reasons, you want someone to know you love them, but you can't tell them with your words. Perhaps they are dead. Perhaps you are estranged. Perhaps others are listening, and your love must remain secret. Whatever the reason, you can send a message of the heart, a pulse of Aphrodite energy, by means of the sacred dove post. This is useful for healing damaged relationships, and building up broken people, but it can also be used to more subtly tug on someone's heart strings, to make your boss like you, or to draw a lover to you, or for almost any other reason.

Make a copy of the ikon. On the back of the ikon, encode your message; I write mine in words, but you could also draw pictures or even just breathe your heart's energy directly into the paper, like a sponge. To level the spell up, use green ink, and scent the paper with roses. Read Aphrodite's hymn aloud, and then pay attention to her while you color her ikon. Have a conversation, or just listen. Roll the scroll, and tie it with a ribbon. Green is best.

---

233 Obviously, the Greek does not say 'smoke of our bowls'. You can replace the last couplet with 'Goddess we call, our words dripping sweet wine, Grant your supplicants' wish, let us bask in your shine' if you prefer.

Next, assume the godform of Aphrodite in the ikon. When you can feel yourself there, give the scroll to the dove, and explain to whom it should be delivered. Respectfully burn the scroll over charcoal, and follow it by burning rose petals and frankincense. Remember to say thank you.

ADONIS

Ἄδωνις

56: ADONIS, LORD DUMUZI

Listen to my call, O daimon most brave,
Beloved Adonis, of lordly good name.
Your luxurious hair spreads out like twined vines,
O king of the solstice, you burst forth, divine,
In the season of growth and joyful encouragement.
You grant us true counsel and multiformed nourishment.
Your lamp is extinguished, along with the green,
And honored with weeping, both seen and unseen.
Androgyne child, both female and male,
Eternal Adonis for whom women wail,[234]
Adonis, two-horned one, you make the plants grow,
O strong, thick-haired huntsman, we reap what you sow.
Much loved, finely formed, and lovely in psyche,
Belov'd sapling child of sweet Aphrodite,
Born to the bed of the Lady of Hell,
In whose holy presence you annually dwell,
Reclining beside her in the dimness of Tartarus,
Then rising up like the sap to the heights of Olympus.
Draw near, blessed one, lord of death and rebirth,[235]
And gift your initiates with the fruits of the earth.

Adonis is a relatively late import from the east into Greek religion. Nearly all modern scholars are in agreement that his myth was greatly influence by the much older myth of Ereshkigal (Persephone), Ishtar (Aphrodite), and Tammuz (Adonis). Adonis' name is the Greek version of אֲדֹנָי (Adonai), which means 'lord'. There is no question that the figure of Adonis is intimately linked, both historically and magically, to Phrygian Attis, Egyptian Osiris, and the Semitic gods Tammuz and Baal Hadad. Functionally, Adonis (like the others I just listed) is a vegetation god. There are many versions of his story. The version below is largely based on Ovid's, although I have also woven in others in an attempt to tell the story for modern listeners.

---

234 This line has no counterpart in the Greek. The tradition of weeping for Adonis is discussed on page 184.

235 The rebirth of Adonis is speculative. In most myths, he's just dead. However, the hymn specifically says that, after death, his body rose to Olympus 'like ripe fruit'. Also, it seems odd to imagine that the daimon of vegetation does not rise again.

On Cyprus, the island of Aphrodite, King Cinyras raped his daughter, the blameless girl Myrrha, and then blamed her for seducing him. This is a story as old as time, and so current it is playing out in your neighborhood right now.

Aphrodite looked kindly on the girl, and transformed her into a tree, so that she could not be further abused. The tree, called myrrh, cries even today, and her tears smell of longing, grief, magic, and death. Myrrha gave birth to beautiful boy, who screamed and caterwauled beneath his tree-mother. The boy was the most beautiful thing Aphrodite had ever seen. She picked him up, dandled him, and nursed him at her own breast. But then, she grew rather bored of him; Aphrodite isn't the mothering sort. She gave the boy to her cousin, Persephone, to raise. There, in the silent darkness beneath the world, the boy thrived, growing more and more beautiful every day. When he was fully grown, he was, undoubtedly, the most beautiful human the world had ever seen. With Persephone's blessing, he walked up out of Hell and into the living world, where Aphrodite saw him again, and she desired him.

Persephone, his adoptive mother, did not approve of this mating. Aphrodite had, after all, turned Myrrha into a tree, rather than just smiting her rapacious father! Aphrodite had, after all, nursed this boy at her own breast! It just wasn't right. It just wasn't natural. And also, it wasn't fair. For Persephone also lusted after the boy, although she would never admit that, or act on it. The laws of the underworld are strange, we are told, but altogether just.

The sides were drawn up, with the Queen of Life on one side and the Queen of Death on the other. The world was coming apart at the seams. Father Zeus intervened, and a compromise was reached. In the dry season of death, Adonis would be with his mother, Persephone, below the world, among the shades, deathless and immortal, and there he would continue to learn at her side. In the wet season, Adonis would be with Aphrodite, as her human lover. And the last third of the year, he might spend as he chose. The two queens agreed to this bargain, and then they told Adonis his fate. Some say that he chose to spend that third with Aphrodite, and some that he spent it wandering the world.

In any case, years passed, with Adonis commuting back and forth from his mother, the queen of Hell, to his lover, the great green goddess. And then, one day, the young man went hunting with his companions, who slew a sow, the sacred animal of Persephone. Adonis gasped in horror and was still gaping in shock when the wild boar's tusks entered into his belly, and he dropped, bleeding, to the forest floor. The laws of the underworld are strange, we are told, but altogether just.

Aphrodite, on Cyprus, cried out in pain. "Adonis is dead! Adonis is dead!" Her tears mingled with his blood and the rich black earth and gave rise to the anemone flower. She taught all the women to weep for him. Adonis died, it is said, that the plants might live.

❊ ❊ ❊

Adonis' primary festival, the Adonia, is generally at midsummer. It was traditionally a women's rite. Women of all classes and cults joined in the celebrations, with noble ladies, slaves, and prostitutes worshipping side by side. Women took to the rooftops, where they sang, danced, and planted Adonis Gardens, growing lettuce and fennel in broken pots, so that they sprouted, then withered and died. The women ritually mourned these, descending into the streets and processing with the withered greens to sacred springs (or, on many islands, to the sea) where they ritually buried them. The phrase 'like a garden for Adonis' is used, to this day, by Greeks to refer to something that will never work.

As the exploited boy, Adonis is unusual in our myths. Our culture has few role models for boys who are exploited and raped. In fact, the taboo on even speaking about such things runs so deep that almost all commentators and scholars, including those who claim to be anti-patriarchy, minimize this part of the story, reducing Adonis to an entirely symbolic and metaphoric figure, or paint him as an expendable creature, unfit for manhood. The scholar Marcel Detienne, for example, in *Gardens of Adonis*, paints him as an anti-Herakles, saying that he "is nothing more than a victim as weak as he is pitiable."[236] This is as offensive as it is absurd. Adonis is powerful, not in spite of, but because of his pain.

---

236 Marcel Detienne, *The Gardens of Adonis: Spices in Greek Mythology*, 2nd edition (Princeton: Princeton University Press, 2021).

HERMES CHTHONIOS

Έρμῆς Χθόνιος

57: HERMES CHTHONIOS, THE UNDERWORLD GUIDE

You who dwell on the banks of the river of lamentation,
From which there is no return to the place of inhumation,
Hermes, son of Dionysus, who dances nightly
With your mother, delightful Cyprian[237] Aphrodite.
You bask in the light of her quick darting eyes,
As you tend to Persephone's underworld shrine,
And attend as a midwife to her yearly rebirth.[238]
Just as you escort our souls to homes under the earth,
Through dire doom, when our fate comes to pass,
With the wand, hypnotizer,[239] you enchant us at last.
You rouse us from our sleep, and wipe webs from our eyes,
Setting our feet on the path where all endings lie.
In the name of Persephone, you act as guide
Along the Stygian path, level and wide,
You lead by the hand eternities of mortal souls,
We beg, send us good death when we've met all our goals.

---

237 The specific place referenced here is Paphos, a city on the southwest coast of Cyprus.

238 This part, about Hermes guiding Persephone back into the world in the spring, is not in the hymn, but would have been understood by any audience in ancient Greece.

239 ὑπνοδῶτιδι (hypnodotidi) or 'she who gives sleep'.

EROS

Ἔρως

58: Eros, Love

I call to great Eros, lovely and pleasant;
Attend to our prayer, come and be present.
Draw back both your wings and your mighty bow,
Let loose the fletched flame, your swift-whistling arrow.
Playful and clever, dual-natured sprite,
Gaming with humans and immortals alike.
You are the key that opens all locks,
The aetheric heavens, the sea, and the rocks,
The pneuma that births all that we see,
Grown from the gift of the goddess all-green,
And all of the things that wide Tartarus keeps,
And the roar of sea, resounding the deeps.
For your hand on the rudder is the guide of the wise,
And so, blessed one, attend to our cries:
Join mystic initiates in immaculate thought,
Drive away the foul onslaught of vile assault.

MOIRAI

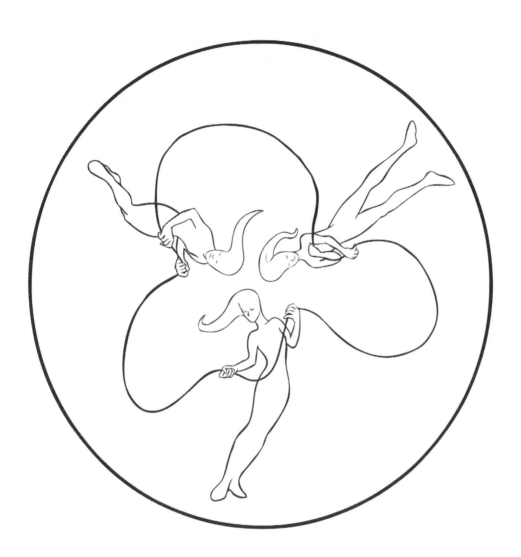

Μοῖραι

59: MOIRAI, THE FATES

Endless and infinite, Beloved children of inky Night,
Fates, providence, Moirai,[240] I call you to our rite!
O many-named ones of the heavenly pools,
Whose warm waters burst forth like shining white jewels,
Everflowing by night, into the grotto,
In the whole holy hole's innermost hollow.
You first bubble forth from spiritual places,
From whence you fly forth o'er earth's boundless spaces,
then, nimble and quick, you scamper on down,
To be with the ancestors, under the ground.
In justice and glory, purple-robed, you drive out,
On the liminal edge between hope and doubt.
From Okeanos,[241] the true ever-boundless boundary,
The primeval origin of everything around me.
Who looks down from on high, to gaze on we mortals?
Only the Fates, and none of the other immortals.
The eye of Zeus, who knows the end of the many-born we,
Fate and Zeus alone know the reasons of all that must be.
But I stand here in the middle, gentle-hearted and kind,
And call out to the daughters of noble father Mind:
O Atropos, Who Must Be!
O Lachesis, Assigner of our Destiny!
O Klotho, Weaver of all that we see!
Nocturnal, eternal, invisible, implacable,
You are indestructible and all-unattackable.
All things you give, and all things you stay,
And you are they who take all things away.
You who are the contingent and the necessary things:
Fates, hear my prayers, and hallow my offerings!
I beg you to attend to your mystics' rite,
Banishing sorrow and advising delight.

---

240 The Greek word here, Μοῖραι, is the plural of μοῖρα, which has a range of meanings not
entirely translatable into English. Μοῖρα can mean a person's individual destiny, but it can also
mean a portion of land, an inheritance, or a share of plunder. Our word 'destiny' or 'fate'
implies a very future-looking concept, but the Greek is more a state of being; the μοῖρα a person
is born into is their assigned lot in life. By extension, it can also mean a division of people, such
as a class or caste. It is perhaps best understood as 'what one is due'.

241 Here, Okeanos is subtly called by his name Ogyges. The Greek reads ὠγύγιον παναπείρονος
εὐνόμου ἀρχῇ.

KHARITES

Χάριτες

60: GRACES

Hear me, O Graces, daughters great-gloried and famous,
of curvaceous Eurynome and good father Zeus:
Aglaia the Splendorous, and Thalia, Good Cheer,
And Euphrosyne, the Mirthful – we call you: Draw near!
Richly blest, well-disposed, joyful, maternal,
All-kind, all-holy, shape-changers eternal.
In all mortal hearts, you excite warm desire,
Your flower-formed faces blush with rose fire.
We pray you come to your mystics, each in her time,
Bringing wealth and great blessings, gentle and kind.

NEMESIS

Νέμεσις

61: NEMESIS, WHO SETS THE BALANCE RIGHT

I cry out to Nemesis: goddess, all-seeing queen,
Who sees into the hearts of all mortal beings.
Eternal one, exceedingly venerable, holy, august,
Delighting in Dike, ally of the just,
Shape-changing shifter, quixotic, dynamic,
Chaotic, confusing, perhaps even erratic,
Your word's ever changing and under discussion –
A long winding road, but arcing toward justice,
For you hear every care in the hearts of mankind,
And the fear of you weighs on each mortal mind,
The overproud psyche, and the promiscuous liar,
Can try to escape you, but finds no safe harbor.
You see all, you hear all, you judge every lie,
Justice dwells in your heart, O daemon most high,
Come, blessed one, mystic friend of the wise,
Give good intent wings, cut down hateful lies.
Replace unhallowed thoughts and contemptuous feeling;
Stop the fickle, flip-flopping wheeling and dealing.
Blessed goddess of fairness, please heed our cry,
And to your task, mighty Nemesis, now fleetly fly.

Nemesis is the Greek goddess of reparations. She is a twin to Tyche, the goddess of fortune, whom we will meet in hymn number 72. Her name derives from the word for 'fair distribution'; Nemesis is the righteous anger that unfairness engenders, and the just retribution that punishes it. Nemesis balances the scales when luck is too unfair.

She is often described as the goddess who punishes ὕβρις (ubris). Although ὕβρις is the origin of the English word 'hubris', they don't mean exactly the same thing. In English, 'hubris' implies excessive pride, but the ancient Greek concept of ὕβρις was different. Ὕβρις covered a wide scope of bad behaviors. Aristotle[242] defined it this way: "to cause shame to the victim, not in order that anything may happen to you, nor because anything has happened to you, but merely for your own gratification. Ὕβρις is not the requital of past injuries; this is revenge. As for the pleasure in ὕβρις, its cause is this: naive men think that by ill-treating others they make their own superiority the greater." In English, I think the best word for that is 'exploitation'.

---

242 Aristotle, *Rhetoric*, 2.2, trans. by J. H. Freese (Cambridge: Harvard University Press, 1926), 1378b.

When she is understood as the goddess that punishes exploitation, Nemesis is restored as a glorious and powerful goddess of the people. That her name, in our speech, has come to mean 'enemy' is a byproduct of how deeply ὕβρις is wound into our culture. So much of our popular entertainment glorifies shaming people for personal gratification; this is the very definition of ὕβρις. We have been trained to believe that Nemesis is our enemy, but she is the goddess who upholds equity and punishes unfair exploitation.

A SPELL TO CURSE IN THE NAME OF NEMESIS

You will need:

- Your target's full name, and a photo of them.
- The ikon of Nemesis on the last page of these instructions.
- Colored pencils, crayons, markers, or another way to color in the image.
- A black pen that won't bleed through the paper.
- A permanent black magic marker.
- Scissors, red embroidery floss, and a sharp needle.
- A white novena candle in a jar.
- About an hour, ideally that of the Sun on a Saturday night.
- $13 dollars in cash.

What to do:

1. Resize the photo of your target so that their face fits in a circle the same size as the Nemesis ikon.
2. Print the ikon out on one piece of paper and the photo of the target out on another.
3. Cut around the circular border of the ikon. Trim the photo to the same size.
4. Compose a letter to Nemesis, explaining the injustice you are asking her to address. Do not specify the punishment, allow her to decide what is fair.
5. Write 'Nemesis' on the candle in the ancient alphabet using the marker.

ΓΕΓΕΣΙΣ

6. Enter into magical time, space, and consciousness in your usual fashion.
7. Search your heart for guilt in the matter at hand. Confess any wrong you have done, and then cleanse yourself in the usual manner. You should only be cursing in a situation where you are the injured party, but few situations are

entirely black and white. If you have any guilt in your heart, that can cause the spell to rebound. Confess and cleanse.

8. Write your target's name, birthday, phone number, address, or any other identifying information on the back of their photo. If you have their hair or other material links, attach them to the photo. While doing this, focus on the idea that this ikon of them is slowly becoming a direct portal to them. When you are complete, say (something like) "Creature of paper, I baptize you NAME, for you are the essence of NAME, and whatever is done to you is done to them."

9. Light the candle.

10. In your most magical voice, read aloud the hymn to Nemesis.

11. Color in the ikon of Nemesis, focusing on the goddess herself, <u>not</u> the situation. You may add any symbols or other artistic details that seem appropriate to you. There is not a 'correct' way to color her; make her yours. If you wish, you may chant her name or her hymn while you color.

12. Write your letter, in black, onto the back of the Nemesis ikon. It is best, but not necessary, to write in a clockwise spiral, starting at 9 o'clock and ending in the middle. If there is extra space, add appropriate magical symbols to fill the circle.

13. When done, read your letter out loud.

14. Using the needle and red thread, sew together the two paper circles, with the letter to Nemesis touching the photo. Leave several inches of thread before your first stitch. I recommend blanket stitch. Sew completely around the edge. Leave several inches of string after the last stitch; tie the two ends together with three knots.

15. Put the package on the table, with Nemesis face up. Put the candle on top.

16. Say *"Nemesis, I charge you, by the time this flame goes out, right the scales of justice. In payment for this, I offer $13."*

17. Sit with Nemesis and listen as well as you can to what she has to say.

18. Return to normal time/space/consciousness in your usual fashion.

Before the candle goes out, distribute the $13 to at least three different beggars. Look them in the eye, smile and bless them (You can just say "Be blessed.") when you give them the money. If you absolutely cannot find 3 beggars, you may instead donate $39 to a charity which supports the unfortunate.

DIKE

Δίκη

62: DIKE, JUSTICE

Celebrate now, with dancing and song:
The all-seeing eye, ever watchful and strong,
Justice, sweet Dike, of fine glowing form,
Who sits on the throne at Zeus' right arm.
Dike, we pray, as you look down from on high:
See all peoples of Earth below the blue sky,
Meet every injustice with truth, as you must,
With righteous avenging, fucking crush the unjust!
When judges lack judgment, when the courts are corrupt,
When decisions are hard, grant prudence. Instruct!
When men tread on justice, step up, say "Enough!"
For you alone can bring justice against the unjust.
You hate those wrongdoers who break public trust,
but look kind on the minds of those who are just.
Goddess, we praise you. Oh Dike, true Justice,
Nourish our souls and continue to love us.

DIKAIOSYNE

Δικαιοσυνη

63: Dikaiosyne, Equality

O holy Equity, blest and beloved one,
Goddess rejoicing in all things rightly done,
You are honored by all, blissful and bold,
Lofty and right-thinking, you cannot be sold
Nor bought, for you are inviolate and all incorruptible.
You break even those who think they're untouchable,
Who in greed would attempt to cheat your great scales,
Unbalancing the right and greasing the rails.
You are dauntless and charming, famous and fabled,
For you rejoice in peace, and a world that is stable.
You loathe the unfair and delight in what's right,
You are the crown of the virtues and wisdom's true light.
Shatter the wicked, mighty Goddess! Thus do we pray:
Destroy evil men and wash all vileness away,
So that all those who nurse from the breast of the Earth,
All who from the deep sea were first given birth,
May follow your path of justice and nobility,
Living in harmony and peaceful tranquility.

NOMOS

Νομος

64: NOMOS, LAW

Holy king, on whom both mortals and deities call,
Heavenly Nomos, who hangs the stars over us all,
You seal the boundary between the earth and the sea,
You secure natural order, judging ever impartially.
Free from factional friction and sectarian strife
You protect those who live a just and lawful life.
As you travel the heavens, you send down from above
The power to root out injustice and replace it with love.
Your strong hand on life's rudder lets us draw our breath,
And you alone guide us mortals to our noble deaths.
You cut the straight and narrow, you are upright forever,
You keep peace among those who live together.
You act with primeval wisdom when you judge the just,
But on those who are wicked, you look with disgust.
Bliss-bringer, ever honored, you ignite our great passion,
Let your memory rekindle my inner compassion.

ARES

Ἄρης

65: ARES, RUIN

Unconquered, strong-spirited, daemon of might,
Indomitable, magnanimous, maker of right,
Delighting in arms, clashing swords are your calls,
Bespattered in blood, you batter down walls.
You find joy in killing; many men have you slain.
Horrid One:
calm your rage,
stop your strife,
cease the pain!
Yield yourself to the wishes of Cyprus' queen,[243]
Yield yourself to the revels on Lyaios'[244] green,
Use the might of your arms to do the work of the goddess,[245]
Let boys blossom in peace, blissful and honest.

---

243 Aphrodite.

244 Dionysus.

245 Deo. Here 'the work of the goddess' probably means 'agriculture'.

HEPHAESTUS

Ἥφαιστος

66: HEPHAESTUS, GLOW

Strong-minded Hephaestus, unwavering blaze,
You bring light to us mortals with all-flaming rays,
You hold high the sun torch in your ever-strong hands
And bring the red light of flame to all mortal lands.
Perpetual artisan, workman, blameless cosmic pyre,
All-devouring, all-taming, all-consuming fire!
Sky, sun, stars, moon, undefiled lights,
Not just the fires of Earth, but those of the heights
Are the gift of Hephaestus to all mortal beings,
Poured out from your cup of infinite blessings.
Every home, every city, every nation praises you,
For our inner soul-fire is kindled by you.
Blazing one, hear our call, come drink your libation,
Help me rejoice in my work, free from temptation.
Stop the fires of rage that burn through my soul,
Ignite blessed joy-glow in hearts that are whole.

ABOUT THE IKON

In our ikon, Hephaestus is shown with a prosthetic/robot hand, tempering a newly forged lightning bolt he has made for Zeus. Although, traditionally, Hephaestus' disability is usually in his legs, we wanted to be sure to picture his difference, even though his legs are out of frame. There are, broadly, two types of stories about how Hephaestus became handicapped. In one version, he was born that way, and was cast out by his mother, Hera, on account of his deformity. In other versions, he is born whole, but injured as a child while attempting to intervene in Zeus' abuse of Hera. For this insolence, he was thrown down from Olympus, crippled by the fall. In both versions, he lands on the island of Lemnos, where he is nursed by clever humans[246] there. In exchange for their care, he teaches them the art of the smith.

A SPELL TO GET A JOB

This spell is a very traditional type of sympathetic drawing magic. You could write a similar spell, with perhaps a different deity, to draw other things to yourself.

---

246 A Thracian people called the Sintians.

You will need:

- If enchanting for a specific job, you will need a copy of the job listing, ideally including the company's logo. To enchant without a specific job, make a list of what you want in a job.
- Scissors.
- Colored pencils, markers, or another way to color in the ikon.
- A black pen. For added power, use iron gall ink.
- A white candle, and a way to light it.
- About 1 oz of olive oil. For added power, add frankincense essential oil.
- A fireproof pot larger than the ikon, and a lid for it. A cast iron cauldron is ideal.
- A dinner plate larger than the ikon.
- About an hour, ideally the hour of the Sun on a Thursday or the hour of Jupiter on a Sunday.
- An outside location. If you cannot be outside, open a window. This spell can produce a lot of smoke.

What to do:

1. Print a copy of the ikon with the job listing (or description) on the back.
2. Using any method you like, enter into magical space, time, and consciousness.
3. In your most magical voice, recite the Orphic Hymn to Hephaestus while looking at his ikon.
4. Turn the ikon over, and then turn it 90 degrees clockwise (so that the top of the job listing is on the right).
5. Use the black ink pen to sign your name, big, over the job listing, claiming it as your own.
6. Turn the ikon face up again, and speak from the heart, asking Hephaestus to help you get the job, and promising that you will endeavor to give an honest day's work for an honest day's wage.
7. While you do this, color the ikon in.
8. Be open and allow Hephaestus to guide you. You may want to include magical words, sigils, or other elements into your coloring.
9. When you are done coloring, read the hymn a final time.

Put the candle in the cauldron (but do not yet light it). Put the ikon on the plate, and pour the olive oil over it, coating it completely. While the oil soaks into the paper, light the candle and then read the Orphic Hymn aloud a third time. Pick up the ikon, and let the excess oil drip off. Light the ikon on fire and drop it in the cauldron. Once the ikon is completely burnt, put the lid on the cauldron.

A SPELL TO KEEP YOUR JOB

This is, at its heart, a binding spell designed to keep a situation the way it is, preventing significant movement. It should be deployed when you have reason to believe your job is in danger. This includes being afraid your hours will be cut, or your job will otherwise get worse. It should not be done without need, because it can also have the effect of preventing promotions, raises, or other good changes in your work situation. Similar spells with other gods can be used to stabilize and reinforce other situations, especially those which involve formal contracts (including marriages). This spell can be refreshed weekly.

You will need:

- A printout of the ikon on top of your employment contract. Print out your employment contract, then run it through again to print the ikon on top, on the same side.
- Colored pencils, markers, or another way to color in the ikon.
- A metal chain long enough to completely encircle the ikon; it's ok if the chain is bigger than the ikon. A cheap necklace chain is fine.
- A white novena candle and a way to light it.
- A clear glass of clean drinking water.
- $5 in gold (colored) coins.
- About an hour, ideally the hour of Saturn on a Thursday or the hour of Jupiter on a Saturday.

What to do:

1. Using any method, enter into magical space, time, and consciousness.
2. In your most magical voice, recite the Hymn to Hephaestus while looking at his ikon.
3. Speaking from your heart, in your own words, explain the situation you are asking Hephaestus for help with. Promise that you will put in an honest day's work for an honest day's pay and ask him to help you keep your job.
4. While you speak with him, color his ikon. Focus on the heat of the lightning and the coolness of the water, and the balance between them. Use hot reds, yellows, and oranges for the flaming lightning bolt and cool blues and greens for the water.
5. When you are done coloring, once again, clearly state to Hephaestus exactly what you want.
6. Put the candle to the right of the ikon, and the water on the left.
7. Light the candle.
8. Take a sip of the water.

9. Slowly, encircle the ikon with the chain, while saying (something like)…

   Hephaestus, worker's helper, master crafter,
   You temper the new-forged blade with water,
   As this chain surrounds your image,
   Lock down my job.
   Lock down my job.
   Lock down my job.

10. Place the coins on the ikon.

11. Leave them for at least a day, but not more than a week, and then distribute them to the non-profit of your choice. Labor unions are a good way to go, as are charities that provide job training. It is best to directly contribute the coins, but you can also donate $10 and keep the coins.

12. You can refresh this spell by simply burning another candle and reciting the spell again.

13. This should be done weekly for as long as the danger of job loss continues.

ASKLEPIOS

Ἀσκληπιός

67: ASKLEPIOS, THE GREAT SURGEON

Asklepios,[247] ur-doctor, all-hallowed life saver,
Spell speaker, ill easer, smooth talking soothsayer,
Shaman, your strong sorcerous song never wavers,
Your charms disarm harm, O pharmaceutical savior.
Inspiring Hygeia to extirpate illness,
Replacing anxiety with blest inner stillness.
You do battle with doom and struggle with sickness;
Blessed bloom bringer, you keep away mischief.
Much-honored scion of Apollo, the pure,
Beloved bed-partner[248] of Hygieia, the Cure,
Enemy of malady, good giver of life,
Bring us hale health and keep away strife.
We beg you walk by our side until our lives' end,
As our steadfast companion and much-honored friend.

---

247 The origin of the name is unclear, but it is likely related to *skallo* (to stir up, hoe, metaphorically to probe).

248 In other, more patriarchal tellings, Hygieia is the daughter of Asklepios, but I believe (as do the Orphic hymns) that he gains his skill from her, rather than vice-versa. Certainly, historically, it makes more sense in that order. See her hymn for more details.

HYGEIA

Ὑγεία

68: HYGEIA, HEALTH

Ever-blossoming queen of all,
Most-blest all-mother, Hygeia, I call.
You banish all injury, affliction, and illness
And cause every home to blossom in bliss.
Every craft lusts after your ordering hands,
With which you reach, ever gentle, to plumb the dry lands,
Saving those souls that Hades would destroy,
And filling up every house with the fullness of joy.
You're hated by Hades, who plunders souls from the living.
Eternally thriving, your prayers are life-giving.
Without your holy magic, your guiding spells,
Human lives drift, bobbing as corks on the swells.
In the absence of you, Plouton's gifts[249] lose their sweetness,
And human old age brings only hardship and weakness.
For you alone hold such power over peasant and king.
Multi-mysterious goddess, your praises I sing,
Defend us[250] from sickness and all leaden pain,
Let us bask in your light and rejoice in your reign.

The hymns to Asklepios and Hygeia are perhaps my most frequently used hymns. They are designed to be prayed for those in need of healing. As a broad rule of thumb, I pray Asklepios' hymn when someone is in critical condition due to an acute injury or when they are undergoing surgery. Hygeia's hymn I find better for chronic and systemic illnesses, and psychological and spiritual healing, and for those in recovery.

Hygeia, whose name means 'health' and is the root of the English 'hygiene' is the great goddess of healing. Her tender ministrations bring us back into right alignment with the world, which the Greeks believed (as I do) to be a necessary precondition for thriving health.

Asklepios, whose name is closely related to the English word 'scalpel', is the Greek god of surgery. The two rarely appeared independently; temples to one were nearly always also temples to the other. Those temples, the Asklepia, were hospitals as well as centers for dream incubation. If you had an ailment your own village healer couldn't cure, you came to one of the great Asklepia to seek treatment from the temple

---

249 Wealth.

250 I pretty much always reword this line with the name of the person I'm praying for. Changing 'defend' to 'save' and dropping the 'all' are the easiest way to make up for extra syllables, but play with it yourself.

attendants, called 'therapeutes'. In an underground chamber called an 'abaton', the patient was instructed in how to seek healing instructions in their dreams. In the night, the god would come and tell them what they must do to get better, and also instruct the doctor-priests.

ERINYES

Ἐρινύες

69: ERINYES, FURIES

Hear me, good goddesses, all-honorable loud-shouting ones,
You scream with the power of ten thousand suns.
Allekto, the Unceasing, who pursues those in flight,
Tisiphone, the Avenger, who sets the scales right,
And Megaira, the Blood Debt, who cries "Never again,"
Erinyes, fierce Furies, cry "Euoi" the Bacchic Amen!
Stealthy and silent, you move through murky gloam,
From slippery-banked Styx, where you make your home.
Good guardians, ever vigilant, of holy right order,
You fly hither and thither policing Good's border.
Naked save beast skins, you are primal and free;
Raging, high minded, you cry out to Necessity.
Avengers most mighty, in pain you suffer and writhe,
Shape-changing maidens who pay Hades' steep tithe.
Through Stygian mist, and mortal aggression,
Run swift and invisible as secret perception,
Implacable and eternal, you guard the numberless tribes,
Overseeing judges, with your fierce Justice-eyes.
O goddesses, multiform, holy ones of the fates,
Your eyes cackle bright, your hair twines with snakes.
Lend me agency and effectiveness, courage, and skill,
Transpose power for frailty, in my heart and my will.

EUMENIDES

Εὐμενίς

70: EUMENIDES, KINDLY ONES

Gracious Ones, hear me, great-named givers of glory,
Eumenides, Erinyes, vengeful phantoms of fury,
Come well-disposed from your dark Stygian grotto,
Divine daughters of Zeus who rules down below
And Persephone, Beloved, with beautiful hair
That flows o'er her shoulders, shining and fair.
You investigate mortals who do grievous wrong,
Avenging injustice, for the right standing strong,
O dark-skinned queens, your eyes flash ever bright,
Your sharp flesh-eating teeth reflecting the daylight.
Hellish and terrifying, you serve no masters or lords.
Your own fierce-willed hearts direct fearsome swords.
The unjust, the wicked, the repulsive bad guys?
You paralyze their limbs like maddening gadflies!
O grim maidens of night, you span all the timelines,
Many-fated, you escape kismet's cruel confines.
Your hair curls like snakes, your hands curl like claws,
I summon you now – Judge by Nature's just laws!

The name 'Erinyes' is of uncertain origin. Hesiod claimed it meant 'strong ones', perhaps from the root *eri* (very). Others point to *orinein* (excite) or *eris* (strife). My favorite folk etymology is *en era naiein* (dwelling in the earth). The Furies are so fearsome that they are rarely referred to by name, instead apotropaic paranyms (euphemistic names used to avoid mentioning evil spirits) are substituted. The most common of these is 'Eumenides', usually translated as 'Gracious Ones'. I prefer 'Kindly Ones' as a wink to the common English apotropaic paranym for those spirits whom the unwise might call 'faeries'.

The Furies are goddesses that punish all wrongdoing, but they specifically curse oath-breakers. Such since are very common in our culture, which does not properly respect oaths. One common situation in which such a curse arises is when a couple has divorced legally, but not unwoven the oaths they swore in their marriage ritual. Thankfully, as long as they are not left to fester, such curses are easy to break, as long as the original oath is known. It is usually sufficient to officially renounce the vow, while making a restitution offering to the spirit(s) that witnessed and sealed the original oath.

If you are already experiencing symptoms of an oath-breaking curse, unweave the oath, make restitution to any humans you've hurt, the witnessing spirits and the Eumenides, make a full confession of how you've broken your word, apologize for disrespecting Those Who Enforce Oaths, take a shower, wash yourself carefully, and then scrub with salt water, from head to toe. After you get out of the bath, declaim hymn number 70, and then go to bed and sleep on it. Record your dreams. If you have a nightmare, repeat the whole ritual. If you've worked this ritual three nights in a row and are still having nightmares, seek expert advice.

MELINOE

Μηλινόη

71: MELINOË, GREEN WITH FEAR

I call Melinoe, chthonic mistress of fears,
Born near the mouth of the River of Tears,[251]
Saffron-robed nymph whose name means 'chartreuse',[252]
You're the daughter of Persephone by Kronian Zeus.
Disguised as her Hades, that treacherous god
Seduced his daughter Persephone in false-hearted fraud.

Her fury red-hot, her heart icy-numb,
Her belly drawn taut, like the head of a drum,
Persephone birthed you, two-formed and terrible,
to drive mortals to madness and frenzy, unbearable.

Slippery shapeshifter, you slither from sight,
Then re-emerge later, shining by night.
When you rise under cover of gloomiest gleam,
I beg you, good goddess, subterranean queen:
dispel psychic gadflies[253] to the ends of the Earth,
And show beneficent face to mystics of worth.

This hymn is hard to translate, not only because the text is tricky, but also because, apart from this hymn, there is very little primary source material about Melinoë on which to draw. She is generally understood to be a goddess of nightmares and ghosts. In the hymn, she is called 'two formed'. I understand this to mean that she has two avatars or faces. In the hymn, Melinoë is beseeched to turn her beneficent face toward the mystic, and turn her terrifying face outward, to dispel psychic attack.

Taylor's translation is more explicit about these two faces. He says of her "Hence partly black thy limbs and partly white, from Pluto dark, from Jove ethereal, bright."[254] This translation has led some modern pagans to syncretize her with the Norse Helle, which I think is a mistake.

Among the few sources which mention Melinoë are a type of bronze triangle. The image below is from Pergamum and was the first discovered in modern times. The tablets appear to have been mass produced; an identical bronze tablet was found in Sardis,

251 Kokytos is more usually translated as the 'river of lamentation'.

252 Μήλινος means 'the color of quince', but it means, figuratively 'sick with fear'. In English, we might say 'yellow-bellied'. Others translate her name as μελας-νόος or black-minded.

253 Madness.

254 Orpheus, *The Mystical Hymns of Orpheus*, trans. by Thomas Taylor (United Kingdom: C. Whittingham, 1824).

and another similar one in Apamea. Around the outside is written "O Persephone, O Melinoë, O Leucophryne", here usually understood as three faces of Hekate. The three goddesses are labeled as Dione, Phoebe, and Nyche (Nyx). Each is labeled Amibousa, which means 'Changing One', probably refering to the moon's phases.

Its function is unclear, but I believe it is a scrying table, with the central disk polished to a mirror finish. Discovered in 1899, and dated to the 3rd century CE, the Pergamum triangle was found along with several other items. Most scholars agree it is a sort of divination kit. Included are a bronze nail, two bronze rings with characters engraved on them, two rectangular bronze lamellae inscribed with characters, three smooth black river stones inscribed with the same characters as the lamellae, and a convex bronze disk inscribed with mystic characters, often called the 'Prognostikon'. In addition to the characters (mostly of unknown meaning) is a circle of Greek vowels: ωιοαη ιεαω υηεω ειοαω ηουι αεηιουω ιηοε. These are most likely 'barbarous names' or magical glossolalia. I was unable to find a public domain image of the whole kit to show you, but you can google 'Pergamum divination kit' and 'Pergamum Prognositkon' to learn more about it.

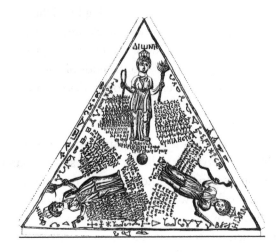

If you would like to experiment with making your own triangle, we have provided a modern illustration you can use. On mine, I place a large glass paperweight in the central circle, which I use as a scrying mirror. You could also use another kind of crystal ball, a mirror (dark or silver), or a bowl of water or other fluid. Additionally, you can put an incense censor in the circle, and scry in the smoke, or a candle in whose flame visions can appear. If you like, you can use the original hymn below to consecrate your triangle:

Hekate, Dione, Phoebe, Nyx:
Mistress of mists that mix in betwixt,
that liminal boundary that guards the Betweens,
Artemis, Persephone, Melinöe, Queens,

By key and by torch, by snake, whip, and blade,
I call to you now: Please come to my aid!
Selēnē, Mēnē, bright moon shine,
Open this portal as Hekate's shrine!
Triple-voiced, triple-headed, triple-faced, triple-necked
Your mirror stands ready, your face to reflect.
Aktiophis, Daeira, give light to true Knowing,
As I bathe this mirror in cold water's flowing,
[pour cold water over the face of the mirror]
And awaken new life as a portal of insight.
Let darkness disperse, giving way to bright light!

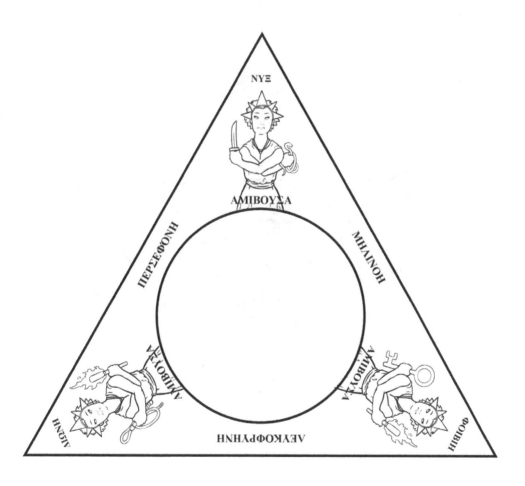

TYCHE

Τύχη

72: Tyche, Fortune

Come, Tyche!
We call you, Enodia supreme,
Sovereign of crossroads, altogether good queen.
Song-renowned daughter of Eubouleus' bloodline:
The good guide who fell, along with his swine,
Through the cavernous crack in the crust of the Earth,
When Kore descended at Persephone's birth.
Tyche, we call in the great name of Artemis:
Gentle essence of fortune, wondrous and marvelous,
Your irresistible wish is fate's sovereign command,
Bring increase in riches and wealth to the land.
Sorcerous and streetwise, you weave the tapestry of fate
with stitches of riches, for those you appreciate.
But those who anger you, you sew into poverty,
Spinning their minds into tangles of anxiety.
Sweet goddess, Eutychia, be my lifelong companion,
Rain down your favor and your nourishing compassion.
Grant happiness, strong-wishing, and generous charity,
Bless our lives and our work with unending prosperity.

Tyche's name is usually translated as 'Fortune', following her Latin name, *Fortuna*. The word 'Tyche' comes from the Greek word *tunkhano* (τυγχάνω), which means to 'hit upon' (i.e., by chance) or to 'happen to be'. Although she has a variety of genealogies in classical mythology, Tyche is often said to be either the daughter of Okeanos and Tethys, or of Aphrodite and Hermes. The first is an echo of an older time when Greece's wealth and luck derived unquestionably from the sea. The second is a more modern conception where luck is a combination of sly cleverness (Hermes) and winning charm (Aphrodite). What is most relevant, I think, is that both of these pairings match a crossroads god with a fertile great goddess. This, then, are the roots of Fortune: Novelty and Fecundity. Likewise, all spellwork with Tyche follows this formula, that the seed of a good idea falls on fertile ground and there flourishes.

Tyche had three main forms. The first, that of Eutychia (good luck), was often depicted holding a cornucopia and the babe Ploutos, the god of wealth (not to be confused with Ploutôn, a name for Hades, the god of the underworld). In her primordial form, Tyche is often depicted with a ball of string, as one of the Moirae, the weavers of fate. Finally, in her dark form, Tyche is Nemesis (whom you met in the 62nd hymn).

While the hymn petitions Tyche as the goddess of personal luck and fortune, in her exoteric cult she was more often portrayed as the embodiment of the luck of a whole community. For this reason, she is often shown in statues wearing a mural crown (a crown made of a city skyline). As imperial oligarchy rose, she became, more and more, a symbol of empire. In this guise, as the anthropomorphic guardian of a political entity, she survived the transition to Christianity more easily than many other deities. For example, the so-called Tyche of Constantinople remained a regular feature of Byzantine art well into the 6th century.

Our ikon focuses on Tyche as the granter of good luck and wealth. She is a fat and happy goddess, full of life and energy. From her infinite cornucopia, she pours forth unlimited blessings of wealth, happiness, and luck. Her mural crown depicts a bustling city skyline, and her long veil covers her face, because luck is so often both hidden and blind.

A Spell for Good Fortune

As the goddess of luck and fortune, Tyche can be partnered with for almost any kind of magical operation. After all, when ISN'T luck helpful? This spell focuses on her wealth-bringing aspect, but it could be adapted for a wide variety of other uses. In this case, I'm enchanting to bring good luck, wealth, and fame to the *Orphic Hymns Grimoire* project, but you can substitute yourself or your business wherever I reference the hymns.

You will need:

- This book
- A special pen[255]
- Paper[256]
- 10 coins, preferably golden[257]
- A small white candle
- A small cup of water
- Frankincense & a way to burn it
- A lit white taper candle (the helper candle)
- A table, ideally with a white or gold tablecloth
- An hour, ideally that of Jupiter on a Friday, while the moon is waxing.

---

255 For this operation, dove's blood ink is ideal, but not required.

256 Fancy paper is great, but plain white paper is fine.

257 I use $1 Sacagawea coins, but quarters or chocolate coins wrapped in gold foil will also work. A pile of actual gold would be ideal, but one imagines people with access to piles of gold should maybe be using their magic to do something more worthwhile than getting even more wealth. Whatever you use, you're not getting it back.

As is the first step in nearly any magic, first decide exactly what you want. When you know exactly what you want, write a letter to Tyche requesting it. Be as artful with the wording as you can, but do not trade off clarity for poetics.

After you've written your petition, kiss it, and lay it face up in front of the open book. Arrange your altar with the book at the back. In front of it, on top of the petition, arrange the 10 coins in a 'tetractys pyramid'[258] as follows: Use 6 coins to make an equilateral triangle pointing at the ikon. Next, use 3 coins to make another smaller triangle centered on top of the first one. Center the final coin on top of that. In front of the coin pyramid, put the votive candle (unlit). To the left of the coins, put the incense (unlit). To the right of the coins, put the (full) cup of water. It's best to set all this up in advance.

Next, enter magical consciousness, time, and space however you see fit. Light the helper candle and use it to light the candle and incense. Dip your finger in the water, and touch it to Tyche's lips, and then your own.

Begin with the Pythagorean prayer to the Tetractys: *Bless us, divine number, who generated gods and men! O holy, holy Tetractys, you contain the root and source of eternally flowing creation! For the divine number begins with the profound, pure unity, growing until it comes to the holy four; then it begets the mother of all, the all-comprising, all-bounding, the first-born, the never-swerving, the never-tiring holy ten, the keyholder of all.*

After awakening the tetractys, pour a splash of the water over the tetractys, then use the helper candle to drip a bit of hot wax on it. Blow the incense across it. When it feels alive to you, continue.

Align yourself with the essence of Orpheus, so that you feel empowered to speak in his name. Stare directly into the (veiled) face of Tyche, and read the hymn aloud, in your most magically powerful voice. In your own words, speaking from your heart, make your wish.

Sit with the ikon, communing with it, watching and listening for a response. You may also use any divination method you like to communicate with Tyche during this time. If you do not receive a clear response in the ritual, seek one in your dreams.

Over the next week, you must give away all ten coins, ideally to ten different beggars. If, by the following Thursday, you still have coins left, you may leave those that remain at a crossroads or throw them into a wishing well or fountain. When your request is fulfilled, you must donate at least $10 more dollars (but more is better) to an appropriate charity. The ikon, with the spell petition on the back, may be ritually disposed of or kept in a petition box.

---

258 The tetractys is usually arranged as a flat triangle of ten points, but in spellwork, it is often arranged as a pyramid. It is rife with symbolism. The single point on top is the Divine Unity. The three sides of the triangle represent the harmony of the Three Worlds. The four faces (bottom + 3 slanting faces) represent the Four Elements, with the stability of earth at the base. The six points of the base represent the six directions: left, right, front, back, up, and down. The ten coins represent the Holy Decad, the base of our counting system.

DAIMON

Δαίμονος

73: Daimon, Great Spirit

I invoke Daimon!
Can you feel the great shudder?
Make open the way for Commander of Thunder!
Gentle Dia, pangenitor, you spark mortals to life;
Great Zeus, all-king, wandering wide.
You bring great abundance when you enter a home,
Teeming with power, great to behold.
But, on the other hand, you also bring pain
Suffering, shivering, life-draining strain.
Both grief and delight are yours to bestow,
So we ask, blessed one, that you send pain Below.
Banish all worries of ruin and strife,
And send a sweet end to an estimable life.

LEUKOTHEA

Λευκοθεα

74: Leukothea, White Goddess

You glitter like diamonds in the sun's midday gleam,
Your seafoam silk scarf afloat on the green.[259]
Leukothea, White Goddess, born Ino of Thebes,[260]
You nursed Dionysus and crowned him with wreaths.
O protectress, most holy, of the deep heaving seas,
We cry out together, we pray: Hear our pleas,
You, who delight in the swells of the silver-tipped waves,
Deliver those sailors being dragged to their graves.
Rescue those mortals from most miserable death,
As the deep cold sea water replaces their breath.
The capricious onslaught that causes shipwrecks,
And the tender salvation of those you protect:
Both arise from your tides, O mighty sea goddess.
We beg, Leukothea, that you graciously bless,
your initiated mystics when they pick up the oars,
Protect them and guide them back to our shores.

Leukothea's name means 'white goddess', an allusion to both mother's milk and seafoam. Leukothea is the savior of the shipwrecked, gently netting them from the waves with her white veil. Among her many epithets is Thalassomedoisa, or 'Sea Ruler'. Pindar calls her "sharer of the sea-nereid's bower".[261]

In the more familiar myths, Leukothea is an ascended mortal. She was, in life, called Ino, the daughter of Kadmos of Thebes. With her husband Athamas, Ino[262] fostered Dionysus, thwarting Hera's plan to destroy him. In retaliation, Hera drove Athamas mad[263] and he killed their eldest child, then came for Ino and their younger son, Melikertes. Ino leapt with Melikertes into the sea, and they arose as Leukothea and Palaimon, gods of the Ionian Sea. Later, she rescues the shipwrecked Odysseus in Chapter 5 of the *Odyssey:*

---

259 These first two lines have no parallel in the original. Leukothea filled my heart with them while I floated, beyond the breakers, in the Atlantic Ocean. You may omit them if you desire.

260 Literally, the hymn calls her 'daughter of Kadmos' (the legendary king of Thebes). However, the tale of Ino (on the next page) would have been known to the audience.

261 Pindar, *Odes*, ed. by Diane Arnson Svarlien, (1990), Perseus, <http://data.perseus.org/citations/urn:cts:greekLit:tlg0033.tlg002.perseus-engl:11>

262 Ino is the sister of Dionysus's mother, Semele.

263 Usually in these Homeric stories, if you replace 'Goddess drove him mad' with 'Toxic patriarchy poisoned him,' the story makes more sense. So why does Homer, the poet laureate of patriarchy, blame it on a woman? Good question.

She it was who now felt compassion for Odysseus the persecuted wanderer; she flew up from the waves as a seagull might, sat on the strong-bound raft... [she said] "And see—this is a scarf of mine, of celestial make; wind it round you above your waist, and you need fear neither death nor harm".[264]

However, there are other stories of Leukothea coming to the sea. In Rhodes, they tell of Halia (Ἁλία), a nereid wife of Poseidon whose name means 'she of the salt'. Halia is the mother of Rhodos, the wife of Helios and goddess of the island of Rhodes. Halia also bore six mortal sons, cruel and wicked boys. When the newborn Aphrodite came to their shores, they refused her entry, and she cursed them with madness. They set upon their mother, raping her. To escape them, she threw herself into the sea, who is her mother, and there she still lives as Leukothea.

Prior to beginning my work with this hymn, I knew Leukothea only in passing. Much of this translation (and the other oceanic hymns) was done while I was on retreat in Ocean City, New Jersey in early August of 2018. Because I am very fair and burn easily, I always wear a light shawl at the beach. On this trip, I was wearing a wrap of white silk shot thru with silver threads. I suspect it is this, and the words of her hymns dripping from my lips into the waves, that caught the goddess' attention. During the days I spent at the ocean, Leukothea came to me very powerfully in my dreams, and taught me many things. When I was researching her further, I learned that at her temple in South Laconia there was a dream oracle. There, she shared a temple with Helios and his daughter Pasiphaea, the sister of Circe.

A Leukothea Spell to be Free of Debt

You will need:

- Two large glass or metal bowls or other deep containers. Bigger is better.
- Salt water. Ocean water is ideal, but any salt and any water will work.
- A tarp, or old towels. They will get stained. This spell makes a mess. You can do it outside.
- A small beeswax poppet of the person who is in debt, including as many links (blood, hair, nails, photos, etc.) as possible, prepared and baptized in the usual way. If your poppet is not beeswax, that's ok, but it must be able float.
- Documents relating to the debt (bills, etc.). (These will be ruined; copies are fine.)
- If possible, material links to the debt holders, such as a rock from the parking lot of your mortgage holder. Promotional materials with the logo of the bank (or other creditor) on them are also good. Credit cards are excellent.

---

264 Homer, *The Odyssey*, trans. by Robert Fagles (London: Penguin, 1997), p.

- A printed ikon of Leukothea & colored pencils (or the like) to color it with.
- A white candle.
- Fresh rosemary stalks.
- Gold (colored) coins. These coins will be blessed during the rite.
- A very thin white scarf or other cloth. A white tea towel will work. It needs to be big enough to easily enfold the poppet. This will be stained (and blessed) by the end of the ritual.
- Black squid ink, which can be bought at fancy gourmet food stores. If you can't find it, use another natural black ink.

Preparation:

1. Read this entire chapter.
2. Make a full accounting of all your debts. Write them down and collect all the supporting data you can.
3. Spend some time thinking about how you got into this situation. Did it happen slow or fast? Was it a medical crisis? Theft? Irresponsible spending? Write a letter to yourself, explaining what happened. Take responsibility and 'make confession' for the parts of it that are your fault, and make sure you've addressed anything that might happen again. Write this down.
4. Write a clear explanation of what you would like to have happen. What would 'salvation' from your debt look like?
5. Arrange some towels under and around the container. This spell makes a mess.
6. Prepare the 'Sea of Debt':
   - Line the bottom of your container with the debt documents and lendee links.
   - Fill the container halfway with salt water.
   - Speak over the water, naming it Sea of Debt. Explain to it that it is the sea of debt in which you are drowning. Name all the debts. Explain how those debts have come to pass, and how they are damaging you, and what you need. Really feel it. If possible, cry into the sea. Spend some time on this step.
7. Prepare the 'Lustrous Water of Salvation':
   - Line the bottom of the second container with your explanation of what you want.
   - Fill it half full of salt water.
   - Speak over the water, naming it Lustrous Water of Salvation. Explain to it what its nature is. What does your situation look like after you are saved? Be specific and use detail. Really feel it. If possible, cry into the water.
8. Arrange the sea, bath, candle, incense, poppet, icon, and colored pencils all within reach of a work surface large enough to color the ikon on. The floor next to the bathtub is my preferred location.

THE RITUAL

- A Sun hour on a Saturday or Saturn hour on a Sunday are good choices for this work.
- As much as possible, make it dark, with flickering light reflecting on the work surface.
- Play ocean sounds.
- Enter magical time, space, and consciousness in the usual fashion.
- Light the incense.
- Chant aloud the Orphic Hymn to Leukothea. Repeat several times until you feel the connection 'click'.
- Color in the icon. The whole time, speak aloud to Leukothea, explaining the situation and asking for help. If no words come, just speak her hymn over and over. Take your time and do a good job. If you wish, you may work words, seals, sigils, or other magics into the illustration as you color. Don't stop talking until you are done.
- Read the hymn out loud again to seal the coloring.
- Write on the back of the hymn, and read it aloud, a petition addressed to Leukothea asking her to save you from your debts. Respectfully submerge the ikon into the Bath of Salvation. Place the coins on top of it.
- Light the rosemary on fire. Let it smoke for a little, and then submerge the rosemary into the Lustrous Water of Salvation to 'activate' it. Speak her name aloud once more: 'Lustrous Water of Salvation'.
- Chant the hymn once more, and then throw the poppet into the Sea of Debt. (It should float.)
- Add squid ink to the Sea of Debt to turn it black and 'activate' it. Speak its name aloud once more: 'Sea of Debt.'
- Beat the Sea of Debt with your fists while speaking aloud your greatest fears related to the debt. Really feel it. When you are crying out, at peak frenzy…
- Abruptly change to chanting the hymn. Chant loud and strong!
- Use the scarf to fish the poppet out of the Sea of Debt, and deposit it into the Lustrous Water. When you drop it, say Εκας εκας εστε βεβηλοι! or *Hekas, Hekas, este beboloi!* which means "Away, away past mundanity!"
- Carefully, gently, and lovingly wash the poppet off.
- Rinse out the cloth in the Lustrous Water. Hang it to dry. It is now blessed by Leukothea. When they are both dry, you can wrap the poppet in it.
- Dispose of the sea of debt. A toilet or garbage disposal is a good choice, but you can also pour it onto the ground. (Remember, it's salty, and not good for plants. Pour lots of extra water to wash it out.)
- Exit ritual time, space, and consciousness as usual.
- Take all appropriate mundane actions to work on your debt.

PALAIMON

Παλαίμων

75: PALAIMON, WRESTLER

Dionysus' brother[265] who dances and leaps,
You lead bacchic revels in the sea's deeps,
I summon you, Palaimon, to our true-holy rite
Come swimming, well-wishing, with child's delight.
When winter winds shiver the timbers of ships,
And the icy-cold storm holds the sea in his grip,
Save those poor souls who are lost on the seas,
Blaze forth as a savior for those in great need.
Guard from the wrath of tempest and wave,
Extend your compassion, O you who save.

---

265 The word here means literally 'one raised with'. Palaimon and Dionysus are cousins and foster brothers; their mothers (Ino and Semele) are sisters. After Semele's death, Ino took in Dionysus and raised him alongside her own son, Palaimon.

MUSES

Μοῦσαι

76: MUSES, INSPIRATIONS

Daughters of Memory and loud-sounding Thunder,
Pierian Muses, glad mothers of wonder,
In the vision of mortals you take many forms
all of them Beloved and greatly adored.
For you are the excellence of true education
That nourishes psyche with learned libation.
You set the mind straight and order our thoughts,
Diagnosing all errors and connecting the dots.
You are the true rulers, the mind's noble queens
Who initiate mystics with cryptic myth-dreams:
Klio, the historian, great granter of fame,
Euterpe, 'Well Pleasing' is your very name,
Thalia, the Bloomer, who brings poems to flower,
Melpomene, Songstress, tragic chorus of power,
Terpsichore delighting in song and in dance,
Erato, who sings the sweet lovers' trance,
Polyhymnia teaching uncountable songs,
And Heavenly Urania, to whom stars belong,
Plus Kaliope, my[266] mother, with the beautiful voice:
Mighty goddesses, ever pure, in whom we rejoice,
Come to your mystics, hallowed and diverse,
O glorious goddesses of holy verse,
Teach us your ways, so that we can aspire
To polyhymnic glory in your mystical choir.

---

266 That is, Orpheus' mother.

MNEMOSYNE

Μνημοσύνη

77: Mnemosyne, Memory

I summon Mnemosyne's all-brilliant gleam,
Beloved goddess of memory, titanic ur-queen,
Consort and lover of Kronian Zeus',
Mother of the musical numinous Muses.
You are free from all trauma that damages soul,
You mend minds and make men whole.
Merciful monarch, empower our minds,
As all of our memories you lovingly entwine.
Treasure forever each thought in your heart,
Awaken our minds! Never, never depart!
Banish forgetfulness from this sanctified rite.
Bless mystic memory and bring truth to light.

Mnemosyne is the Titaness of memory, and the mother of the Muses; you might know her name from the English word 'mnemonic'. Her name comes from μνήμων, which means 'memory'. That word comes from the Proto-Indo-European word *men- which means 'to think' and is the root of the English word 'mind'. Memory was the seminal art of mind in ancient Greece and understood as the foundation of all arts and sciences. Mnemosyne is not just the goddess of memory, as we moderns understand it, but of the Art and Science of Mind: the mother of Inspiration. Mnemosyne's hymn was the first one I translated, and in many ways, this book is owed to her.

Some modern sources give the folk etymology Menai Mossun, or 'Moon Tower'. While there is very little ancient connection between Mnemosyne and the moon, it is a delightful idea, and one I think Mnemosyne would endorse. The moon is the ancient calendar-keeper, and the Moon rules over the human perception of time. Like all the Titans, Mnemosyne is a goddess of Time. Memory is our faculty to perceive the past, just as prophecy is our faculty to perceive the future, and Mnemosyne, who inspired the great oracles, rules over both of those things.

Even if we understand the connection between Mnemosyne and the moon, what does it mean that she is the 'tower of the moon'? Among her Titan brothers, four are held out as the Pillars of the Earth. Koios, whose name means 'questions', is the Pillar of the North, just as he is Thuban, the ancient pole star. Hyperion, the father of Sun and Moon, is the Pillar of the East, the gate of dawn. Iapetus, related to the biblical Japheth (son of Noah), is the Western Pillar. Finally, Krios, the Ram, whose rising on the southern horizon marked the beginning of the Greek year, holds up the South. If we understand Mnemosyne as the Tower of the Moon, what does that make her sisters?

The usual Latin name for Mnemosyne is Moneta. Some people will tell you that there are two goddesses named Moneta, She of Memory, and Juno Moneta. However, as I understand it, there is a goddess, named Moneta, who became syncretized with both Mnemosyne and Juno. Moneta's name may derive from the Latin *monēre*, which means 'remind',[267] or it may derive from the Greek *moneres* (μονήρης), which means 'solitary' or 'unique'.

No matter where it came from, Moneta's name is undoubtedly important to you. The temple of Juno Moneta in Rome was also the mint and treasury of Rome, and our words 'money' and 'mint' come from her name. Money keeps a record of barter; it is the 'memory' of the economy. In fact, the following words all share a common Indo-European root (*men): <u>Mnemosyne's</u> <u>mental</u> <u>money</u>, <u>memory</u>, is the <u>momentum</u> of <u>mind</u>.

Mnemosyne is the goddess who inspired the oracle of Trophonius in Lebadeiam, Boeticia. Trophonius[268] began as a god of beekeeping. Legendarily, he[269] built the temple of Apollo at Delphi, but died shortly thereafter. Many generations later, the village of Lebadeiam was suffering from a plague. They sent a messenger to the oracle at Delphi to ask what they should do. The oracle told them that must find the cave of the lost hero of Lebadeiam, Trophonios, and properly honor him.

When word came back to Lebadeiam, the whole town tried to find the cave, but it was only discovered when a boy followed some bees through a small tunnel and became possessed by the spirit of Trophonios. The people of Lebadeiam soon cured their plague and gained a popular oracle.

An Offering Rite for Mnemosyne

This rite can be used to worship Mnemosyne, or to call her presence forth for oracular or other spell work. It is useful, but not required, as a preliminary working before all of the rest of the spells in this chapter. If you wish to establish an ongoing relationship with Mnemosyne, perform it each full moon.

You will need:

- Frankincense or another resin
- A white candle
- Two glasses of cow's milk, in which you have infused 11 star anise
- Two small offering cakes. I use koulourakia, a type of Greek cookie.[270]
- An ikon of Mnemosyne

267 And sometimes also 'teach' or 'warn'.

268 His name means 'nourisher'.

269 Along with his brother Agamedes.

270 There's a recipe in the appendices.

What to do:

1. Clean and prepare yourself and your space.
2. Enter into magical space/time/consciousness by any method.
3. Arrange the altar with the ikon facing you, with the candle and frankincense (still unlit) in front. Put the milk on the right and the cakes on the left.
4. Lift up the ikon, and kiss Mnemosyne. If this is your first time, kiss your fingers, and then touch your fingers to her hand. If you have already established a more intimate relationship, do what seems right to you.
5. Light the candle and incense.
6. Speak from your heart, saying something like: "Blessed Mnemosyne, goddess of memory, I offer to you the smell of this frankincense [*smell it*] and the light and warmth of this flame [*Put a hand between you and the candle and move it, letting the light shine through your fingers. Feel its warmth on your palms.*] I offer you, oh moon-white cow of heaven, the richness of milk [*taste the milk*], and the sweetness of this cookie [*taste the cookie*]. Please come and be with me."
7. Read out loud the Orphic hymn to Mnemosyne.
8. Spend some time in Mnemosyne's company.
9. Speak from the heart, saying something like "Thank you Mnemosyne for your wise counsel. Stay as you will, go as you must. The channel is closed."

A POTION TO IMPROVE MEMORY
Based on PGM I 232-247

1. Prepare a potion of the mingled waters of seven springs or fountains.
2. Burn the following and collect the soot on a lid.
   • 4 drams (1 Tbsp) myrrh
   • 3 Turkish figs
   • 7 date pits
   • 7 scales of a pinecone
   • 7 stalks of 'single stemmed artemisia' (I use *artemisia vulgaris*)
   • 7 feathers of Hermaic ibis[271]
3. Dissolve the resinous soot in alcohol to make Hermaic myrrh ink. Make extra ink, we'll use it in other spells.
4. On priestly papyrus[272] write the following:
   ΚΑΜΒΡΗ ΧΑΜΒΡΗ ΣΙΖΙΩΦΙ ἈΡΠΟΝ ΧΝΟΥΦΙ
   ΒΡΙΝΤΑΤΗΝΩΨΡΙΒΡΙΣΚΥΛΜΑ ΑΡΟΥΑ ΖΑΡΒΑΜΕΣΕΝ
   ΚΠΙΦΙ ΝΙΠΤΟΥΜΙ ΧΜΟΥΜΑΩΦ ἈΚΤΙΩΦΙ ΑΡΤΩΣΙ
   ΒΙΒΙΟΥ ΒΙΒΙΟΥ ΣΦΗ ΣΦΗ ΝΟΥΣΙ ΝΟΥΣΙ ΣΙΕΓΩ ΩΙΕΓΩ

---

271 I use goose feathers, because they are used as quills.

272 Or slick, heavy paper.

ΝΟΥΧΑ ΝΟΥΧΑ ΛΙΝΟΥΧΑ ΛΙΝΟΥΧΑ ΧΥΧΒΑ ΧΥΧΒΑ
ΚΑΖΙΩ ΧΥΧΒΑ ΔΗΤΟΨΩΘ ΙΙ ΑΑ ΟΟ ΥΥ ΗΗ ΕΕ ΩΩ

5. Wash the text off into the mingled waters.
6. Drink a dose of this potion on an empty stomach for seven nights at moonrise.

A CHARM TO ACHIEVE A GOOD MEMORY
PGM II 41-42

"Draw a cartouche on a five-fingered plant with myrrh ink and keep it in your mouth while you sleep."

The text does not specify what sort of five-fingered leaf to use. Betz translates it as cinquefoil, but I do not think that is right. The usual Greek word for cinquefoil is 'pentaphyllon' (five-leaf), but the word here is 'pentadactyl botana' (five-fingered plant). Also, cinquefoil leaves are very small; too small to write on, I would think. I believe the plant in question is juvenile marijuana. However, I do not usually have access to whole marijuana leaves. Instead, I write the cartouche on a small piece of papyrus, and then soak it in oil.

AN AMULET TO IMPROVE THE MEMORY
PGM III 412-423

The amulet can be made in three phases, if you don't want to do it all at once.

Phase One:

1. By night, engrave the following name of the soul of the god onto a silver tablet, ideally with a copper pen:[273] ΕΙΚΙΖΙΤΕΑΙΘΑΕΘΦΥΣΟΥΣΚΑΖΗΤΘΖ

Phase Two:

2. Say aloud over the tablet:
   I, NAME, arise from Tohu wa Bohu, the first darkness.
   Closed-mouthed and dark-sober.

---

273 Ink on paper also works.

I have died and yet live.[274]
I have passed the gates of Hell and arisen again.
Like Jesus,[275] *the Great One, I arose.*

3. Put a bowl on top of the tablet and use it to mix cow's milk and barley meal to form a dough.
4. Mold it into 12 small goddess figures, and bake them.

Phase 3, which should be done on the night of a new moon:

5. Fast from when you awaken until moon rise.
6. Go outside and face east.
7. Pour out an offering of cow's milk to the Goddess.
8. Eat a cookie, savoring it, and offering the taste up to the Goddess.
9. Take the tablet in your hands.
10. Kneel, and cover your face with the tablet, writing toward you.
11. Say the follow formula seven times:

> *Borka, borka.*
> *Frix, frix, rix.*
> *Ach, Ach.*
> *Amixag ooch thip.*
> *Lai Lai Lamlai. Lam Mailai.*
> *Aah*
> *Eee*
> *Aye*
> *Ooh*
> *Mou Mou*
> *Oh Ee Oh*
> *Nak Nak Nak*
> *Lainlim Lailam*
> *AEO*
> *OAE*
> *OAE*
> *EOA*
> *AOE*

---

274 If this isn't true, you shouldn't say it. Instead, stake some other claim to magical authority, for example by reference to an initiation. For example, a Christian friend suggests this for those who have been baptized: "By my baptism in Christ Jesus, I have died and risen again with Him." You could also stake an ancestral claim. For example, Jews could say "I am an inheritor of the line of Abraham, a child of the house of the Jacob". If you have successfully completed the Orphic initiation in the appendix, you can call on that "I am Mousaious, and I speak in the name of Orpheus".

275 You can substitute 'Orpheus' if you prefer. I do.

EOA

OEA

Enter, leader, into my psyche and grant me memory.

MMM

EEE

Methef

12. Kiss the tablet.

13. Move the tablet so its lower edge is at your third eye, and the words face out.

14. Run your right thumb from the tip of your nose, up the bridge, and across the tablet.

15. Wear or carry the tablet all the time.

16. Every month, at the new moon, bow to the moon and show your respect.

RECOVERING PAST LIFE MEMORIES

In the Orphic cult, Mnemosyne was most important as the goddess of past life memories. In this context, she was most commonly understood in her river form, and the companion river to Lethe (the river of forgetfulness). Initiates are taught that the most important thing is, upon your death, DO NOT PANIC, but instead recite "I am a child of Earth and Starry Heaven, but my essence is of Heaven alone. This you know. I am parched with thirst and am dying; but quickly grant me from the Waters of Memory to drink."

If you wish to attempt to recover memories of your past lives, first, be really sure you actually want that. The overwhelming majority of the memories you recover are likely to be traumatic ones of your own death. Thus far, I have experienced drowning, burning to death, murder-suicide, and being ritually sacrificed. Those are all memories I could have done without. However, I have also remembered past initiations into magical currents. If you decide you would like to work with your past lives, here is a technique to try to recover them.

1. Sit in front of a mirror, with a single candle between you and it.

2. Play white noise or another ambient sound[276] to drown out other noises and to 'carry' you in the Other Place. Set it to play for 45 minutes, and then stop. When the sounds stops, you are done.

3. Enter into magical space/time/consciousness.

4. Begin with the Mnemosyne offering ritual, but when you get to 'spend some time with Mnemosyne' …

---

276 I recommend this ambient noise by audio engineer Stéphane Pigeon: <https://mynoise. net/NoiseMachines/anamnesisSoundscapeGenerator.php>.

5. Speak from your heart, asking Mnemosyne to nourish you with her healing waters and aid you in recovering memories of your past lives that will help you in your present lifetime.

6. Focus all your attention on the candle flame flickering on Mnemosyne's face.

7. Drift into a very deep trance.

8. Close your eyes and follow the sound deeper and deeper within yourself.

9. Continue to descend into the Underworld.

10. If no guide appears, call Hermes Chthonios, or Hekate.

11. Find your way, with the aid of your guide, to the Halls of Persephone.

12. There, you will find, to the left of the gates, a sparkling pool, with a white cypress tree growing out of it. DO NOT DRINK!

13. Instead, look into the pool and ask to be shown the way to the waters of Mnemosyne.

14. When you reach the river, say (something like) "*I am the child of Earth and starry Heaven; but my race is heavenly; and this you know yourselves. I am parched with thirst. Give me quickly refreshing water flowing forth from the lake of Memory.*"

15. Drink from it, and then look into the surface of the river to see a memory of a past life. You may find yourself pulled into the memory, reliving it. DO NOT PANIC!

16. If you are inexperienced at trance, you may have difficulty with this. If it does not work, ask Mnemosyne to send you a memory in a dream, and work on developing your trance journey skills.

EOS

Ἠώς

78: Eos, Dawn

Hear me, light bringer, bring in the new day,
Awakening sky with your bright beaming ray.
Roll back misty covers, and climb out of bed,
Eos, sweet Dawn, come paint the world red!
Hyperion's[277] herald, Titan all-seeing,
When you rise in Saïs,[278] that easternmost gleaming,
You send black robed Night gloomily fleeing
Under the earth, for her daily sleeping.
You are the glue that holds mortals fast,
To our life and our art, our work and our craft.
You rejoice in the voices of all mortal kind,
No one can hide from your vision on high.
When you shake the sweet sleep from your delicate eyes,
All creatures rejoice, looking up to the skies.
Every beast, from all phyla, from every species,
Those that slither or fly, those under the seas,
All living things work under your gaze.
Shine bright on our shrine and bring light to our days.

---

277 The Titan pillar of the East; the father of Helios, Selene, and Eos. His name means 'Most High'. He is closely syncretized with Helios in later myths.

278 Egypt's capital during the 26th dynasty (664–525 BCE) which is possibly when the original oral versions of the hymn were composed. Legend has it that the tomb of Osiris is in Saïs, and Greeks understood the city to be a sort of antediluvian Athens.

THEMIS

Θέμις

79: Themis, Good Order

I call great Themis, child of Earth and of Sky
Who first spoke as oracle in the recesses of Delphi:
On Pythian ground, above the bubbling spring,
You taught the young Phoibos to be a just king.
You are honored by all, bringing justice's light,
For you first taught us mortals of worship's delight,
You initiate mysteries and you tell us the stories,
And you howl for Bacchus, with infinite glories.
Come, blessed maiden, attend our mystic rites,
And rain down your favor on your acolytes.

BOREAS

Βορέας

80: Boreas, Cold Wind

O wet, wintry wind whipping through space,
Thick with white frost you picked up in Thrace,
Boreas, who washes all strife from the air,
Your wet trailing ooze flows here and then there.
Blow, rain-birther, drop your wet, weary load,
And bring fine, clear weather to your airy abode.
Let the fire-tailed beam of Helios' great glow,
Shine down from the heavens on Earth down below.

In the Orphic hymns, there are only three winds, whose essential quality is not their direction but their season. As we discussed in the chapter on the Horai, the Greek agricultural calendar has three seasons: Blossoming, Growing, and Dormancy. Their winds are, respectively, Zephyros, Notos, and Boreas.

Boreas, the cold wind, generally blows in from the North or Northeast, bringing snowstorms with him. The etymology of his name is unclear; it may be related to an Indo-European root, gʷerH, relating to mountains.

ZEPHYROS

Ζέφυρος

81: ZEPHYROS, TWILIGHT WIND

Zephyros, wander-whisper, ever-dulcet breeze,
Brisk blustery wind born on the wide open seas.
You bring to us mortals deep, peaceful sleep.
Across the spring meadow, you swish and sweep,
from the wavering wheat to the billowing beach.
For you do the sailors beg and beseech,
since you gently guide ships in from the sea.
Quick-witted air, blow big-hearted and sweet,
Unblemished and perfect, mild and meek.
You blow the dawn kisses, and you wave to greet
The dew-clad morning meadow, verdantly neat.
Invisible, ethereal, floating on wings made of light,
O air-shaped Zephyros: Come, nimble sprite!

L ike the other winds, Zephyros is generally associated with a direction, in his
case, the West. His name likely comes from the work *zofos* (ζόφος), which means
'darkness' or 'deep gloom'. This may be because the sun sets in the West. However,
it is also possible that it is meant more in the sense of 'shade', because Zephyros is the
wind that brings the cooling breeze. He is the god of spring, and the consort of Khloris
(the Green Goddess) with whom he fathered Karpos (Fruit).

NOTOS

Νότος

82: Notos, Wet Wind

Swiftly leaping through the lower air,
Rush over the waters. Dart here and there.
Your powerful wings carry moisture everywhere
For Zeus granted you the gift of wandering on air.
Ancestor of the storm, progenitor of the rain,
You gather up the clouds and let them go again.
Please open your heart to the thirsty Earth.
We pray to you, accept our libation in mirth,
And pour out ripening rains that bring fruits to birth.

The word *notos* (νοτος) means 'south' in modern Greek, but it is likely that usage comes from the name of the wind, rather than the wind being named for the direction. Most scholars agree that the name is of pre-Greek origin, but some postulate it derives from *notis* (νοτίς) which means 'wet'. Certainly, Notos is the 'wet wind', the one which brings rain. In Greece, such winds come most often from the south-west, but, to the Greeks, winds are defined by their character, and not really by their direction.

To use this hymn to call rain, stand somewhere with an unobstructed view of the southern horizon, ideally at dawn. Light frankincense and pour a full glass of water onto bare earth. Read the poem aloud three times, and then strike the ground with a staff (or stick). Ideally, the staff should be of thunderstruck oak,[279] but any large stick should work. Depending on local conditions and magical talent, it can take up to a week to work. Repeat the spell each day until it rains.

---

279 That is, from an oak tree that has been struck by lightning.

WINDS

Ἄνεμοι

OKEANOS

Ὠκεανός

83: Okeanos, Primal Ocean

Imperishable ocean, to you we now call,
Eternal Okeanos, undying father of all.
Gods and humans both arise from your infinite flow,
for all things above begin deep below.
You encircle the earth with great heaving surges,
Eternal blue depths where every river converges,
Wellspring of water nymphs, source of the sea,
Birth waters of the Earth, awesome and holy.
Hear us, O blest one, sumptuous divine purifier,
and rain down on our planet all we require.
Your watershed reaches the ends of the Earth,
Your encircling boundary is death and rebirth,
Great Father Ocean, grant your initiates' plea:
Gift your favor forever, as vast as your sea.

Okeanos is generally said to be the firstborn son of Gaia and Ouranus, although in some tales, he self-created (like Gaia), arising out of primordial Chaos before time began. He is place and god in one, the great river-sea that encircles the world, the sea-river into which all water eventually flows. The sun, the moon, the planets, and the stars all lie inside Okeanos' embrace. From his eastern reaches, the sun daily rises, and into his western waters it recedes at night. He is the outer boundary of the universe; beyond him, there is only the dark, cold, expanse of Chaos. Okeanos represents the boundary between the known and the unknown.

Originally, some scholars say, Okeanos rules over the Mediterranean, with Poseidon the god of the Aegean. Over time, as Greek navigational technology improved, and their geography became more accurate, Okeanos expanded to the Atlantic, while Poseidon ruled the inner seas. Today, Poseidon rules all but the deepest, least explored reaches of the earthly seas, while Okeanos is the uncharted depths, both the darkest crevices of the oceans, and the inky depths of outer space. However, it is important to remember that he is not a personification of any place in our world, because he is not fully of our world at all. Okeanos stands at the boundary of our world and the Other Place, he is not so much *of* the hedge as he *is* the hedge. In battles for supremacy here, such as that between the Olympians and the Titans, Okeanos stays neutral. And yet, he is the protector and defender of life on Earth, standing guard between us and the outer darkness. All liminal spaces are his.

Thales, whom Aristotle calls the Father of Science, taught that Okeanos, here not just the mythological figure, but Archetypal Water, was the source of all that is. Aristotle tells us in the *Metaphysics* that...

Thales, the founder of this type of philosophy, says the archê [first principle] is water, for which reason he declared that the earth rests on water, getting the notion perhaps from seeing that the nutriment of all things is moist, and that heat itself is generated from the moist and kept alive by it (and that from which they come to be is a principle of all things). He got his notion from this fact, and from the fact that the semina [seeds, also semen] of all things have a moist nature, and that water is the origin of the nature of moist things. Some think that even the ancients who lived long before the present generation, and first framed accounts of the gods, had a similar view of nature; for they made Ocean and Tethys the parents of creation...[280]

Okeanos has many other names. One of his names is Ogygios (’Ωγύγιος) which means both 'primeval one' and 'giant'. Under this name, or sometimes as Ogyges,[281] he is the first sacred king of Boeotia and Attica (the central region of mainland Greece, including Thebes and Athens). During his rule, there was a Great Flood, which Plato says took place in the 10th millennium BCE, and which so devastated the region that they were without a king for centuries, until Kekrops came to rule, and the 'history' of Athens began.

Okeanos is often simply called 'Old Man of the Sea', a title he shares with many other sea gods and spirits, notably Proteus, with whom Okeanos is often syncretized. He appears in both the *Odyssey* and the *Arabian Nights* as an ancient shapeshifter who obliges young men to carry him on their backs.

And yet, as often as he is a person, Okeanos is also a place: the great sea at the edge of the world. Within Okeanos' waters are the witching islands: including the white island of the West, called Albion (England), and Aeaea,[282] where dwelt the Witch Queen, Circe. Okeanos is also the home of Erytheia, the Red Island of Sunset, the home of giants (and later, of Spaniards). The Gates of the Sun lie within his boundary, and the Land of Dreams lies on his outer shore. He is the headwaters of the Nile and the Danube, and into him flow the four rivers of Eden. He waters the garden of the Hesperides. The Styx, the great river of the underworld, draws its water from Okeanos. He waters the Elysian Fields, the resting place of heroes, but the Dry Lands of the unremembered lie beyond his reach.

In *Prometheus Bound*, Aeschylus has Okeanos give the best of all advice to Prometheus, and to all of us:

---

280 Aristotle, *Metaphysics*, 983b19-31. We now know that all life on Earth did, in fact, began in the primordial oceans, just as Thales taught.

281 Josephus, the chronicler of Jewish legend, tells us that the world tree (some say Oak, but others Terebinth), under which Sarah (the wife of Abraham) gave prophecy in Hebron was also called Ogyges. Josephus Flavius, *The Antiquities of the Jews*, I 10.4 (N.p.: Wilder Publications, 2009).

282 It is unclear if Aeaea is a real place or not. Many equate it with Cape Circeo on the western coast of modern Italy, and other with Cyrpus.

...Although your brain is subtle, you must learn to know your heart, and as the times change, so too must you adapt, for it seems there is always a new ruler among the gods, and so the rules are always changing... Quiet your mind, and do not speak too hastily. Wise as you are, don't you know that a wanton and idle tongue brings only sorrow?[283]

When depicted in human form, Okeanos usually appears as an old man, strong and noble, with flowing white hair and horns. Some say they are bull horns, but I always see crab claws. Sometimes, his lower body is snake-formed, as is the case with many other Old Powers of the Earth.

SPELL CRAFT: OKEANOS' RIVER OF PROTECTION

Sometimes, there are people who are bad for us. Sometimes, it's their fault; they're malicious, evil, and want to do us harm. Sometimes, it's less intentional; they're broken and full of poison, which is leaking out onto you. However, no matter the reason, there are times when you just want to keep a person away from you. You don't necessarily want to hurt them, but they need to keep the fuck away, physically as well as energetically/spiritually/psychologically. This magic is designed to create a sort of 'restraining order' that keeps them and their shit away from you and yours. It's important to include your home and loved ones in the mix, because otherwise, there is some danger that badness aimed at you might splash off onto someone else.

The way I've constructed this particular spell, anything headed your way is deflected into the nearest body of running water, there to be washed out to sea. It's effective against most kinds of malicious magic, but particularly proof against stuff that arises from 'hot' emotions like anger. There is almost no risk of damage to the person whom you are protecting yourself from, and also little risk of 'blowback' onto others in your vicinity, since the work is grounded into the water and eventually washed out to the sea. This work is not recommended for people who live in the desert.

In this charm, we call on Okeanos to create a circle of watery protection around you, a circle of running water that the 'restrained' party cannot cross. Any energy they send your way (intentionally or not) falls into the boundary river, and is washed out to the sea, where it diffuses (and de-fuses) into the depths. This spell is worked with the ikon. You should color your own, as you are moved to do so, each time your cast the spell.

In order to cast this spell, you will need:

- A copy of the black and white ikon above.
- Crayons, colored pencils, or markers.

---

283 Translation from E. B. Browning, *Prometheus Bound, and Other Poems: Including Sonnets from the Portuguese*, Casa Guidi Windows, Etc. (New York: C. S. Francis, 1851).

- A pen with black or blue ink.
- A small bowl of salt water (ocean water is ideal).
- A small white candle (a tea light is perfect).

Using the pen, write your name on Okeanos' chest, as though you are held in Okeanos' arms. Encircling you, the ouroboros snake of protection, and Okeanos' river, which is the root of all water on earth. Outside the circle, write the name or description of whomever or whatever is threatening you. It cannot cross the ring of water. Any spellwork or energy they send your way is trapped by the water, diverted into the groundwater, and thence washed out to sea.

Color in the ikon, using the time to connect with Okeanos through his ikon. Speak to him while you color, telling him about the situation you are asking for help with. Speak from your heart, in your own words. When you are done coloring...

Align yourself with the essence of Orpheus, so that you feel empowered to speak in his name. Read the hymn aloud, in your most magical voice. Next, place the candle on top of your name, within Okeanos' arms. Dip your fingers in the saltwater, and trace along the circle of the ouroboros snake, beginning at his head and proceeding clockwise. Be sure to get the whole circle wet, which may require wetting your fingers several times. Once you've got the whole circle wet, wet your fingers one last time, and make at least three complete circuits without picking your finger up, while saying aloud (something like):

Okeanos, sea snake that encircles the world, encircle me, my home, my family, and my livelihood in your mighty waters, protect and defend me from all attack. Any incursion by those that threaten me, send it away. Sink it to the deepest depths, let it diffuse into the water, and lose all of its power. If my enemy comes by, turn them away. If they ill-wish, let the wish be diverted into the waters. If they curse, let the curse be drowned at the bottom of the sea. Do no harm to my enemy, but turn them, and all their works, away, away, away! They cannot cross your encircling boundary, they cannot cross your running waters. Any ill wish, any energy at all, if it comes from my enemy, turn it aside, and give it to the waters.

Your daughters, the Maidens of the Springs, dew drop clad, with hair of seafoam splash, let them ensnare it in their spider-silk shawls, let them sink the tangled mess into the waters below. Its fires all are gone out. Let it pass through the ground and be grounded, let it rish and rush, burble and bubble down through the streams, rubbed clean and smooth and safe, like sea glass, all its sharpness gone, transformed into a thing of beauty. Let it wash out to the waters and be gone. Let it come to rest at the bottom of the sea, cold and beautiful, a glittering magical treasure that can do no one any harm. There let it rest until it is found, and let it be a blessing on the finder.

Okeanos, Lord of the Great Waters Below, Lord of the Great Waters Above, Great Water Who Encircles the World, encircle me in a river of protection, and keep me safe and whole and strong.

HESTIA

Ἐστία

84: HESTIA, THE HEARTH

Hestia, queen, worthy daughter of Time,[284]
Ever-flowing fire, inferno sublime,
Inhabiting ever the heart of the home,
You walk the initiate into the unknown.
You hallow our spirits with your mystic decree:
"The hearthfire at home IS the flame of all mystery!"
Goddess most wealthy, wise, happy and pure,
Grant us your blessings, we mortals implore.
Eternal shapechanger, basis of everything,
You excite tender longing for the green of the spring.
Your red-tongued smile and your warm glowing eyes
Bless with health, wealth, and happiness
all of our shrines.

Hestia's name literally means 'Hearth', and she both tends and embodies the sacred fire at the heart of every home. When humans first learned to tame fire, Hestia came into being. When fire alone held back the ice, that was Hestia. When flame alone held back the darkness, that was Hestia. She is light, safety, warmth, and life itself. Anthropomorphized as the first-born daughter of Kronos and Rhea, she is a virgin goddess of domestic order, the daughter who stayed home to tend to her aging parents, the spinster who teaches her goddaughters to bake.

As you doubtless recall, Kronos swallowed each of his children as they were born but regurgitated them after Rhea tricked him into a swallowing a stone, instead of the infant Zeus. Hestia, having been the first to be born from Rhea, was the last to be reborn from Kronos, and this first/lastness is important to her mystery. She is both young and old as she chooses, she is the first-born and the last (as Zeus is the last-born and the first). To her is offered the first taste of every sacrifice made in the home, and the last libations of wine at every feast. She is a perpetual virgin (that is to say, she bore no children), and tends the sacred fire of Olympus. Her Homeric hymn says that in the dwellings of gods and mortals alike she has the highest honor.

Unlike Hephaestus, who began as a god of primal natural fire, such as that of volcanoes, Hestia is a goddess of fire that has been tamed to human purpose. Similarly, she is the goddess of that force which tames the natural world, turning it to human usefulness. In this capacity, she is the goddess of domesticity, architecture, and the proper functioning of both home and the state. Of the young gods,[285] Hestia is among

284 Although, as we discussed in his hymn, Kronos and Chronos are not, originally, the same god; by late antiquity they were deeply and irreducibly syncretized.

285 Those who preside over human inventions.

the oldest. When the first human lit the first intentional fire, she came to birth. When you look in the flame, and see vision, there she is. When you come in from the cold, and warmth envelops you in its healing embrace, that is Hestia too.

Hestia is not a human-focused goddess; she tends the eternal flame of the immovable altar of the Heaven, and thus rarely partakes in earthbound drama, which so frequently embroils her siblings. She is rarely pictured, but when she is, she most often appears as a woman in simple robes, with her head covered, sometimes holding a staff.

HYPNOS, PASITHEA, & ONEIROS

Ὕπνος, Πασιθέα, & Ὄνειρος

85: HYPNOS, SLEEP

Hypnos, all-king, you rule both gods and men.
Every creature acknowledges you as sovereign.
You nightly bind our bodies in organic chains,
Driving away worry and soothing all pains.
You bring an end to work, and grant surcease of sorrow;
No matter how bad it is, it can be better tomorrow.
Memento mori, you save souls with every breath,
For you are born from that same womb as Oblivion & Death.
Hypnos, ever blessed one, please come kindly and bright
And mingle with initiates at our mystic rite.

A CHARM AGAINST BAD SLEEP[286]
based on PDM xiv 706-710

1. Pack a jar with dried dates, diced.
2. Fill the jar with just enough cow's milk to cover. Almond milk is inferior, but acceptable. Grain milks (oat, peas, rice, soy, etc.) are not acceptable.
3. Allow to sit, refrigerated, overnight until the dates are mushy.
4. Pour entire jar in food processor, and blend until smooth.
5. Form into balls (easier if you chill it first).
6. Drop one ball into a glass of warm wine or milk and drink at bedtime.

For extra potency, boil eight whole star anise in the milk first to infuse it. Drink the milk with the date-ball. Don't choke on the date-ball. For maximum potency, simmer the star anise and some ground marijuana in heavy cream, strain, and mix some of the cream into milk. A small crock pot is best for this, as it needs to simmer at a low temperature for a long time.

PASITHEA

Pasithea, whose name means 'All Vision', is the youngest of the Graces, a daughter of Aphrodite by Dionysus, the wife of Hypnos, and the mother of Oneioros and the Oneioroi. She is a goddess of trance, and is related to the ancient Minoan Poppy Goddess, whose poppy crown she wears in our ikon. There is not much about Pasithea in classical literature; I know only two myths about her: there is a story where Hera sells her to Hypnos as a bride, and another wherein, during a weaving contest between Aphrodite and Athena, Pasithea spins Aphrodite's wool.

---

286 Insomnia, nightmares, etc.

Pasithea is a goddess of all types of altered states of consciousness, ranging from relaxation and meditative states the whole way to deep trance and hallucinatory states. Personally, I associate her most closely with the hypnagogic trance – the liminal state between wakefulness and sleep. Below is a guided make believe for relaxing and opening yourself to dream and vision. In this make believe, you will imagine yourself to be in the bed she shares with Hypnos. This make believe is also good to help you sleep if you are having trouble.

Pasithea's Bed Make Believe

It is easiest to do this make believe in your own bed, but it can be performed anywhere, especially once you are good at it. Both your physical and inner eyes should remain closed for the entire time. Among the many virtues of this make believe is that, because it is entirely non-visual, practicing it helps build your other inner senses. If visualizations begin to arise before your closed eyes, gently dismiss them, and return your attention to your other senses, and to the feeling of being in Pasithea's bed.

Close your eyes, and connect to your breath. As you breathe in, know that the air you breathe in was exhaled by the trees and plants, and that your exhalations give them life. The air you are breathing connects you to every other living thing. All life shares in the cycle of respiration; the eternal breath of the Earth. Feel the air around you. The air is cool and slightly damp, refreshing and comfortable. A slight breeze caresses you, carrying the scent of forest and river. It is dark, the velvet black surrounding you like a lover's embrace. No light can enter this cave; it is always and ever and always unseen, but deeply, deeply known.

You are snuggled into a soft bed. Enjoy the silken smoothness of the sheets. Feel the comforting weight of the linen covers. Stretch your body. Wiggle your toes. Take delight in your body. Smell the clean, bright, slightly floral scent that lingers on the bedclothes: jasmine and pine and an herb you can't quite identify, green and fresh and magical. Smell the flowers that twine around the bedposts and form a thick carpet around the bed: morning glories and hops, night blooming jasmine, poppies, marijuana, mugwort and valerian. Smell the smoke of the fireplace, redolent with cherry and applewood. Hear the fire hiss and crackle. Listen to what it has to tell you. Perk up your ears to hear the water cascade at the cave's entrance, from whose fountainhead the lazy Lethe burbles her distant lullaby, carrying every care away.

Know that you are safe here. This is the bed of Trance & Sleep, and you are here as their honored guest. Imagine them tucking you in, kissing your forehead, keeping all the monsters away, watching over you like loving parents. Together Hypnos (Sleep), and Pasithea (Trance), have a child, Oneiros (Dream), as pictured in our ikon. Like all Dreams, Oneiros is both singular and many. In the hymn on the following page, they are addressed in the plural, as Oneiroi.

ONEIROI

86: ONEIROI

O blessed messengers of shadowed wing,
Dreams, great prophets who teach everything.
In the quiet sweetness of sleep, you rouse mind and soul
Speaking the future to those who give over control.
Let Good win the race within mortal minds,
For Good brings pleasure to all humankind.
Send holy Dreams that choose to reveal
How to ease the heart and how the soul to heal.
The end to which the godly come is always for a blessing,
Not nightmares which impious men consider so distressing.
O blessed Dreams, please show me what I should do,
So as not to walk the path bewildered and confused.
Do not show me weird apparitions or any evil sign,
As I make nightly visitation with the Oneiroi most divine.

THANATOS

Θάνατος

87: THANATOS, DEATH

I call out to you, Thanatos, for your ever strong hand
Holds the wheel of the ship that crosses dry land.
You pass out pure time, to each one his due,
From that far away moment when they were new,
Until your final slumber shivers their soul,
Dragging their bodies into your black hole,
For you offer liberation from the shackles of physics,
And open the locks of bodily prisons.
You bear every mortal to our eternal rest,
Your power universal, holy, and blest.
Beyond even justice, you are common to all,
For all that goes up, must eventually fall.
You cut down the young just as they ascend,
For you alone decide when mortal lives end.
You are resolute in the face of pitiful prayers,
And persuasive entreaties fall on deaf ears.
Yet, I ask, holy one, dilate time with your weight,
I know you draw near, but I pray that you wait,
I plead with you now, with my offering and vow
"I will live my whole life in the fullness of now",
So grant me that gift which many despise:
Allow me to grow old, and enduringly wise.

There are times, in our culture, when those who are ready to die are not permitted to do so. There are times when, as priests, we are called to help people die well. For such people in such circumstances, I recommend replacing the final three couplets with something like:

Yet I ask, holy one, come gentle and kind,
Bring release and surcease, so I leave pain behind,
Grant the sweet peace of death for my body and mind.

APPENDIX I
WRITING ORIGINAL ORPHIC HYMNS

In addition to changing the ancient hymns to suit your needs, I encourage you to write your own hymns, using the Orphic hymns as inspirational examples. For the most part, the Orphic hymns are constructed according to a template, and basically involve four phases, not all of which appear in every hymn:

1. Epithets: magical nicknames chosen to help 'target' the specific version of the spirit which you want to call. In the Orphic hymns, this is nearly always the majority of the text.
2. Historiola: snippets of myths and stories about the daimon in question. They are chosen to show that the thing you are asking of them is similar to things they've done in the past.
3. Offering(s): Usually this takes the form of "I have lit incense for you" or "I have poured out libations in your name". In the Orphic hymns, this section is normally very brief and straight-forward, if it appears at all. The hymn itself is the offering in most cases.
4. Request: the final phase, wherein you explain what you want.

This is a *very* common format in ancient Mediterranean prayer and magic. If you are familiar with the oeuvre, you might notice that there's a piece missing. Usually, in such prayers, there is usually also a section that suggests why the daimon being called should listen to you. In the case of the Orphic hymns, this is not present, but implied; they listen because you call with the authority of Orpheus, who went below and rose again.

In the example below, I have tried to narrate the process by which I constructed an original hymn for Euros, the Hot Wind. It is designed to inspire more than instruct. Take what seems useful to you and discard the rest.

EXAMPLE: EUROS

As we discussed with Boreas's hymn, there are usually only three Greek winds. However, because many modern practitioners choose to work with the winds as a directional foursome, I have written a new, original, hymn to Euros (Εὖρος), the East Wind, with which you can experiment. We have also provided a second version of the ikon of the winds, which includes Euros.

Phase One: Gather Epithets & Historiolae

The first step in writing an original Orphic hymn is to gather a list of epithets and historiola from classical sources. The website Theoi.com is one excellent source for this.

- Euros (Εὖρος)
  - * Some say this derives from Eos ('Ἡώς) which means dawn
  - * I think it more likely comes from euros (εὖρος), which means 'width' or 'breadth'
  - * There is a possibility of a pun with 'euros' (European money)
- "The wing of red fiery Euros"[287] (Nonnus, *Dionysiaca* 3. 55 ff)
- "hair dishevelled with the blasts, and tawny with too much sand; they drew the tempest on, and in thunderous advance together drive the curling waves to shore, and stir not the trident's realms alone, for at the same time the fiery sky falls with a mighty peal, and night brings all things beneath a pitchy sky. The oars are dashed from the rowers' hands; the ship's head is turned aslant, and on her she receives the sounding shocks; a sudden whirlwind tears away the sails that flap over the tottering mast ...Now Euros (the East Wind) lashes and turns the ship this way and that" (Valerius Flaccus, *Argonautica* 1. 574 ff, trans. by Mozley)[288]
- "Savior of Sparta" (Greek Lyric V Folk Songs, Frag 858 [from Strasbourg papyrus], trans. by Campbell) (B.C.)[289]

Because so little is available about Euros, I had a lot of leeway to design the hymn unconstrained. What we know about Euros is that he is hot, angry, bad for sailors, and blows in the autumn from the south-east. Examining the actual winds present in the Aegean, I have determined that Euros is most likely the wind we today call by its Arabic name; 'sirocco'. Sirocco is a hot wind which originates in North Africa, picking up moisture as it crosses the Mediterranean. The character of this rain is in keeping with the stories of Euros, and it blows into the Aegean from the southeast.

The sirocco is known to carry large amounts of red dust, gathered from the sands of North Africa. This made me think that it might be connected to Set, the Egyptian god of storms and the red desert, and a personal favorite of mine. In Egypt, Set is the Lord of the South, however, Euros is a wind of the southeast, as much as of the east, and south of Egypt is surely southeast of Greece. For that reason, I began to consider Set's epithets, and whether some of them might apply to Euros as well. Among his names are 'Lord of the Desert', 'Powerful One', 'Mighty Armed', and 'Red Lord of the Red Land', all of which felt applicable, so I added them to my list of potentials.

---

287 Nonnus, *Dionysiaca* 3. 55 ff

288 Valerius Flaccus, *Argonautica*, 1.574, trans. by Mozley.

289 Aaron J. Atsma, 'Euros', *Theoi Project* (2017) <https://www.theoi.com/Titan/AnemosEuros.html>

By the time the sirocco gets to western Greece and Italy, it has picked up a lot of moisture from the sea. The moisture mixes with the red dust and becomes the 'bringer blood rain', surely a magical epithet if I ever heard one! Because of its dustiness, the wind is said to cause emotional irritability and health issues. Because of this, I added another traditional epithet of Set, 'Sower of Confusion' to my list. As I read more about it, I was struck by its similarity to the Californian Santa Ana winds, which also blow in from the east, hot, dusty, and terrible. Although Santa Ana is (probably) not actually named after Satan, the word play is irresistible, both for me and for everyone else who calls the Santa Ana the 'Devil Winds', another brilliant magical epithet. I once heard a meteorologist call them 'Caliente aliento de Satanás' or 'Hot Breath of Satan'. Since Set is also very closely associated with Satan, I added that to my list as well. That gave the following list:

- Euros
- Fiery red wings
- Hair dishevelled with the blasts
- Tawny with too much sand
- Sudden whirlwind
- Wind of storm
- Turbulent one
- Tossing ships on the sea
- Lasher of ships
- Savior of Sparta (this is more properly a historiola, which I will discuss further below)
- Kedem (Hebrew for east, used as a name for the scorching east wind in Torah)
- Sirocco
- Simoom (Palestinian name for Sirocco)
- Khamsin (Egyptian name for Sirocco; it means 'fifty' because the wind blows for fifty days)
- Sower of Confusion
- Red Wind
- Lord of the Desert
- Powerful One
- Mighty Armed
- Lord of the Red Land
- Bringer of the Blood Rain
- Devil Wind
- Hot Breath of Satan

Reading over the list, I opened myself to the daimon, and allowed my creativity to flow. That produced a new list of possibilities, some of which wandered a bit too far afield. However, like in all creative processes, it's better to start with too much in the brainstorming phase, and narrow it down later.

- Whistling
- Hiss spitting
- Sandstorm with eyes of fire
- Whip-whirling ifrit
- Hot one of the desert
- Light-bringer. Dawn-singer. Ruddy with dawn.
- Carriage of flame
- Father of wildfire

Next, we'll go looking for historiolae. Because Euros doesn't have much in the way of mythology, these are pretty few and far between. The papyrus which refers to him as the savior of Sparta is only a fragment, and the full story is unknown. Because of this paucity, I've looked to nearby cultures for input. In Bereshit (Genesis), Jakob dreams of a famine blown in by the east wind. In Shemot (Exodus), the east wind brings the plague of locusts, and later parts the sea. In several other biblical settings, the east wind is associated with the withering of crops, and is generally understood as a very bad omen.

Finally, we investigate offerings and requests. Because this is intended to mirror the other hymns to the winds, I've chosen to parallel their offerings and requests. They only barely mention offerings (simply 'libations') and they straightforwardly request the wind to simply appear. However, since this wind seems generally undesirable, I have instead chosen to ask him to be calm.

Phase Two: Rough Draft

Everyone has a different process for creating art. If you already have one that works for you, then you can probably skip this entire section. However, if you don't write poetry very often, I encourage you to experiment with my method, and see how it works for you. I begin by setting the mood by choosing some music. In this case, I wrote under the influence of a 'Hearts of Space' episode entitled 'Desert Winds', which you can listen to at <https://v4.hos.com/programs/details/883>. I layered that music over an animated recording of Saharan winds, which you can listen to at <https://mynoise. net/NoiseMachines/saharaWindNoiseGenerator.php>.

Next, I set to smolder some frankincense, myrrh, and cinnamon, with just a tiny hint of brimstone, and settled into work. Finally, I recited the hymn to the Muses (hymn number 76), as I often do when I am preparing to write.

An Orphic Hymn for Euros: Rough Draft

Euros, East wind, mighty armed power
Your sand laden breaths burnish and scour.

Light bringer, revealer, your wings fiery red,
You bring to birth the ship-whipping whirlwind.
Your hair all in tatters, your skin blasted tawny,
You rush the Sahara and then whip up the sea,
Red Lord of the Desert, Simoon of the Sands,
Sirocco drips blood rain from vast ancient hands.
Devil wind, hiss-whistling in from the east,
I beg you, be calm, stay your rage, be at peace.

Phase Three: Take a Break, and then Edit Mercilessly

Before attempting to edit your hymn, put it away for a while, and get out of your head.

I have a lot of practice at this. Your first draft might be rougher. In mine, there are still plenty of little things to fix. Here's the final version:

Euros, East wind, fearsome armed power
Your sand laden breaths burnish and scour.
Red Lord of the Desert, Simoon of the Sands,
Sirocco rains blood from red desert lands.
Your hair all in tatters, your skin blasted ruddy,
You rush the Sahara then beat the sea bloody.
Light bringer, dawn singer, fiery wings of the morning,
You whip up the ships without any warning.
Devil wind, hiss-whistling in from the east,
I beg you: Be calm. Stay your rage. Be at peace.

WINDS

Ἄνεμοι

APPENDIX II
WORKING WITH IKONS

Coloring Ikons

The ikons in this book are intended to be colored, either by hand or digitally, however you can also use them as is. First, a small bit of business to get out of the way: the ikon illustrations are copyrighted. They may be copied and used in any respectful fashion for your personal practice. If you publish your colorings (including on social media), please include a link to www.OrphicHymns.com. If you wish to use them for any commercial or public purposes, you MUST be granted permission by the illustrator, who can be reached at Chase@MastrosZealot.com

Personally, I like to color a new ikon each time I work with the hymn. I find that coloring is an excellent way to gently enter into the ikon's current, in preparation for working with the daemon in question. I often weave sigils, seals, sacred names and words, and other magic into the coloring. I sometimes color by hand (usually with colored pencils, but I also paint them sometimes), and sometimes I manipulate them digitally in photoshop. I think they would be amazing embroidered.

Most often, I print one out, color it in with colored pencils while chanting the accompanying hymn, and then use the colored ikons for spellwork by writing a petition on the back, and burning candles on top of it. Some I fold up small and carry as talismans. Once you've colored several paper ikons, you might want to make a more permeant wooden ikon, either using the ritual described below or one of your own devising.

Traditional Greek Ikon Practice

There is a rich tradition of ikon practice in modern Greece, where ikons depict deified folk heroes (saints) and other figures of the Orthodox church. Traditionally, when venerating a modern Greek ikon, there is a special procedure. First, cross yourself, and then bow to it. Cross yourself and bow again. Cross yourself a final time and then kiss the ikon. Most typically, the hands of the ikon are kissed, but sometimes the feet are also kissed.[290] In mainstream practice, it is entirely inappropriate to kiss an ikon on the lips, but it is sometimes done without the priests' approval, particularly by witchy old grandmothers. When I venerate the ikons in this book, instead of making a cross, I touch my heart, then my lips, then my forehead, and then bring my hand down, palm

---

290 This is why, sometimes, you see metal 'shields' over the hands and feet of ikons.

up and out, as if I'm blowing a kiss from my third eye. Because the ikons are small, I usually kiss my fingertips, and then touch them to the ikon's lips, and then back to mine. Sometimes, in magic, I put a drop of wine or honey on my fingertips and touch that to their lips. But, most importantly, after veneration, look the ikon directly in the eyes and just listen.

If you would like, it is easy to make your own traditional style ikons. There are a variety of ikon styles, and I encourage you to experiment with your own. These instructions are modeled on a particular Greek style of ikon painting called 'Prosopon'[291] which you can research online to learn more. Before beginning to create your ikon, you'll want to practice coloring the ikon several times, figuring out where you want shadows, highlights, and so forth. Look up images of Greek ikons to get an idea of how the highlights work. How closely you choose to follow these instructions is entirely up to you. They are presented purely as inspiration; my personal ikon making style is inspired by, but not at all the same, as this method.

In the example below, I will talk about painting Hekate's ikon, but the instructions are largely the same for any of the ikons. If you only make one ikon, I recommend Hekate's. As the goddess of magic, liminality, and the first Orphic hymn, she is the 'gatekeeper' of the mysteries. More literally, her ikon can be placed by your front door as a literal protective gatekeeper. Such an ikon is called a 'Hekataion'.

Begin with a flat piece of wood and a photocopy of the ikon sized to fit. You may wish to choose an appropriate wood for the daemon in question. Yew is an excellent choice for Hekate. Paint one side of the wood with white gesso. Before moving on, meditate on the whiteness of the board. In the Orthodox tradition, this represents the eternal light of the Divine, which existed before time. Tape the image to the wood and use an ice pick or burin to trace the image onto the ikon, scoring the lines into the wood, so they will remain visible as you paint.

Greek ikons traditionally have gold backgrounds. If you are not a skilled crafter, I recommend using gold paint on top of red paint for this. However, if you have clever hands and experience leafing, you can use real gold leaf over a thin clay called 'bole'. Whichever method you choose, the first layer should be brick red. Meditate on the redness. In the Orthodox tradition, this represents the red clay from which Adam was made. Personally, I understand it to be the red clay of the Earth Mother, from which all life arises. Allow the red layer to dry, and then you are ready to apply the gold. Meditate on the goldness, which represents the breath of Spirit which animates the clay and gives life to the body.

While the gold dries, prepare the rest of your paints. If you are crafty, you will want to mix your own egg tempura paint the traditional way, but purchased acrylic paint is also fine. If mixing your own, carefully separate an egg, keeping the yolk intact. Save the whites for cooking, and carefully puncture the yolk into a bowl, removing the skin of the yolk. Mix in powdered pigments, then mix in dry white wine[292] to get

---

291 This word means 'person' or 'portrait'.

292 Small amounts of magical potions or oils can also be mixed in at this stage.

the thinness you want. Like every other step, this process is full of symbolism for both Christians and Pagans. The egg is a symbol of life, and it is sacrificed to give life to the spirit of the ikon. The golden yolk represents the sun, which warms the earth and makes all life possible. Finally, by puncturing the yolk, you release the hidden treasure within, never seen by anyone but the god that formed it. The symbolism of the different colors, and the precious materials from which they are made, is ancient and splendid, but too diverse to go into here. For each color you mix, you should meditate on what it means to you. I like to speak aloud to the paints, awakening them to their higher purpose.

Whether you are mixing your own paints or not, ikons are painted in a very particular way. Traditionally, the first thing to be painted would be a red outline on the halo, but since most of our ikons are not haloed, we'll skip this step. Next, apply a dark olive color[293] for the skin. This represents the material nature of the body. Next, fill in her garment with a dark brick red, representing the fire that warms the blood. Use small circular brush strokes, which represent Chaos-Chasm, the first thing to exist at the beginning of creation. You will want to leave a bit of texture on the paint. When this base coat is dry, use a very fine brush (or a fine-tipped marker) to go over all the lines, especially the folds in her garment and facial features.

Mix much lighter versions of the olive and red and use those as highlights over what you've already painted, adding shading and dimensionality. The closer an area is to the front, the more highlighting it should get. Work slowly, and in layers. The highlighting should cover about two-thirds of the figure. This first highlight stage symbolizes the light of Creation, bringing order to the cosmos. When your highlights are dry, move on to the next step.

Apply a thin wash of brighter colors over each area. I like to use pink for the skin and yellow for the robe. This wash should make the ikon appear luminous, but not change the underlying color too much. This represents the light of the spirit, shining through the material ikon. Next, add a second highlight, called the Anthropos, which is the light of human intellect, and represents the divinity the gods acquire through worship. On the clothing, this should go diagonally across the first highlight, producing a faceted effect. On skin, it should blend into the first highlight. Examine some pictures on the internet to get the hang of it. When the highlight is dry, apply a second wash, giving more shine to the spirit within. The Anthropos is what gives many Greek ikons their particular 'vibe'.

Finally, add a third highlight, representing the spiritual light of the divinity. These should be small lines, reinforcing and embellishing the existing highlights. Add a final wash, in a different color, adding further spirit to your ikon.

When all the paint is dry, use a small brush to fill in the remaining details, such as the headdresses and tools. Use a very fine brush or fine-tipped markers to redraw the

---

293 While modern Greek ikons are almost entirely olive-skinned, the ikons in this book are intended to portray the gods in a wide variety of human forms from all over the world. Color their skin however seems best to you.

lines, keeping the edges smooth and clean. Next, add tiny white glimmers and sparkles on the clothes and fine lines on the skin, especially around the eyes. Finally, paint in the eyes, bringing the ikon to life. This is the 'Proposon' of the light of the god. Meditate on how the whiteness of the eye is the same as the board you began with, the divine light of uncut creation. Allow the icon to dry very thoroughly, ideally in direct sunlight. Finally, coat with a clear, high gloss varnish. Traditionally, an oil varnish called 'olifa' is used, but this is a difficult process that is best learned in person. I recommend high gloss acrylic varnish. You can mix very small amounts of enchanted oil into the varnish before applying it. If you use too much, the varnish will cloud, and ruin all your hard work. Test the varnish on a piece of scrap wood you have painted before applying to your ikon.

APPENDIX III
RITUAL OF ORPHIC SELF-INITIATION

*This rite, which is built from the Hymn to Mousaios, should only be undertaken once
you have great familiarity with the contents of this book, and have decided that you want
to make the Orphic hymns a core part of your religious and magical practice. It has the
possibility of making permanent[294] changes in your destiny in this life and those to come.*

*This rite should be performed every day for 36 days, ideally just after a purifying bath and
just before sleep, so that it incubates revelatory dreams. Each day, the recitation becomes
longer; the full hymn is recited on the last three nights. It must be recited from memory.*

*Set up a small altar for this work in your bedroom. Minimally, you need a small glass of
water and an image of Orpheus, before which you should light[295] candles and frankincense.*

- Begin by taking several deep breaths and collecting yourself. Enter into magical time, space, and consciousness by any method.
- Take a deep, full breath, and then...
- Bellow out "EI AI OAI!"
- Breath in, and then out.
- Yell: "Come to me, O god of gods! The Bull who begets the Serpent! The Serpent who begets the Bull!"
- Breathe in again, as deeply as you can, and then close your eyes.
- Roar like a bull as loud and long as you can, and when you are out of air....
- Squeeze out the very last bit, ending with a snake's hiss.
- Repeat this breathing (in, pause, roar-hiss, pause) until you achieve the altered state it brings.

---

294 Personally, I do not actually believe in the existence of 'permanence'. I really mean 'long-lasting'.

295 Here and everywhere else, if you are in a situation where fire is not appropriate (such as a dorm room, prison, or etc.), then do what's right for you and your exact situation. In magic and ritual, candles are nearly always an offering of light and heat, and incense is an offering of pleasure and breath. There are many other ways to make that offering. Close your eyes, and experience darkness. Open them and experience the light. Move your hands in front of your face, drawing in the light, delighting in the both the light and the shadows. Offer the gods the sight of your eyes, and the heat of your body. Can't burn incense? If possible, substitute the same plant in oil form; frankincense has chemical properties that help open the mind to trance. Cigarettes are another good choice; tobacco smoke is an excellent offering. If you can't do that, offer the gods the smell of something else nice: perfume or spices are good choices. If you can't do that, offer the gods the power of your breath and the pleasure of being alive.

- When you are ready, open your eyes and recite from memory the following verses.

Each day, memorize one new couplet of the Hymn to Mousaios, and add it to your daily recitation. Recite the full hymn on three consecutive nights. After the final recitation, repeat the bull-serpent breathing until you feel the power enter you (or you pass out). If you pass out, you'll need to start over.

APPENDIX IV: OFFERING COOKIES

LILLIE MASTROS'S (1924-1999)

Koulourakia are a kind of Greek butter cookie, typically made on Holy Saturday, and eaten Easter morning. They are often shaped into crosses, twists, or circles. In my family, they are shaped like S's which we call 'snakes'. When I was little, I was told that was because our ancestors used these cookies as offerings in their pagan worship of snakes. So do I.

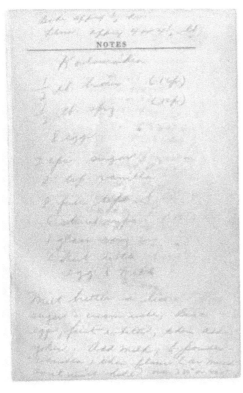

Ingredients

1/4 cup butter
1/4 cup shortening[296]
2 eggs + 1 yolk
3/4 cups sugar
1 tsp vanilla
2 tsp baking powder
2 shots warm milk
Flour: about 1 lb

Cream fats and sugar, beat in the eggs, first whites, then add yolks. Add milk, baking powder, vanilla, then flour (as much as it will hold). Form the cookies. Mix an egg yolk with some water, and wash the tops. Bake at 325°F for 15-20 minutes.

As I mentioned, these can be formed into many shapes, although I especially like making snakes. Many people add orange zest, and/or coat them in sesame seeds or slivered almonds, but I learned to make them plain.

---

296 Aunt Lily's recipe calls for 'Spry' which is an old brand-name for vegetable shortening.

BIBLIOGRAPHY

TRANSLATIONS OF THE HYMNS

Athanassakis, Apostolos, *The Orphic Hymns: Text, Translation, and Notes* (Scholars Press for the Society of Biblical Literature, 1977)

Athanassakis, Apostolos and Benjamin Wolkow, *The Orphic Hymns* (Johns Hopkins University Press, 2013)

Dunn, Patrick, *The Orphic Hymns: A New Translation for the Occult Practitioner* (Llewellyn Publications, 2018)

Hermann, Gottfried, *The Book of the Orphic Hymns Together with the Principal Fragments Also Attributed to Orpheus. The Whole Extracted from Hermann's Edition of the Orphica* (Nabu Press, 2010)

Long, Asphodel, 'Orphic Hymns', Asphodel-Long.Com (2022) <http://www.asphodel-long.com/html/orphic_hymns.html>

Ovid, 'Book X' in *Metamorphosis*, trans. by A.S. Kline (Ann Arbor,: Borders Classics, 2004)

Reihe, Diederichs Gelbe, *Orpheus: Altgriechische Mysterien*, Neuausg Edition (E Diederichs, 1982)

Taylor, Thomas, *Hymns and Initiations: Translation of the Orphic Hymns and a Treatise on Orphic Theology* (Prometheus Trust, 1804)

GENERAL SOURCES

Alesina, Alberto, Paola Giuliano, and Nathan Nunn, 'On The Origins Of Gender Roles: Women And The Plough', *Quarterly Journal of Economics*, 128.2 (2013), <https://scholar.harvard.edu/files/nunn/files/alesina_giuliano_nunn_qje_2013.pdf>

Alexander, Christine, 'A Wooden Hekataion of the Hellenistic Period', *The Metropolitan Museum of Art Bulletin*, 34.12 (1939), *JSTOR*, pp. 272-274 <https://www.jstor.org/stable/3256233>

Aristotle, *Rhetoric*, 2.2, trans. by J. H. Freese (Cambridge: Harvard University Press, 1926)

Atsma, Aaron J., 'Euros', *Theoi Project* (2017) <https://www.theoi.com/Titan/AnemosEuros.html>

Betz, Hans Dieter, *The Greek Magical Papyri in Translation*, Volume 1 Texts (Chicago: University of Chicago Press, 1996)

Bremmer, Jan, *Initiation into the Mysteries of the Ancient World* (Walter de Gruyter GmbH & Co KG, 2014)

Browning, E. B., Prometheus Bound, and Other Poems: Including Sonnets from the

Portuguese, Casa Guidi Windows, Etc. (New York: C. S. Francis, 1851)

Brumfield, Allaire, 'Cakes in the Liknon: Votives from the Sanctuary of Demeter and Kore on Acrocorinth', *Hesperia: The Journal of the American School of Classical Studies at Athens*, 66.1 (1997), 147–72 <https://doi.org/10.2307/148477>

Burkert, Walter, *Ancient Mystery Cults* (Harvard University Press, 1989)

Burkert, Walter, *Babylon, Memphis, Persepolis: Eastern Contexts of Greek Culture* (Cambridge: Harvard University Press, 2004)

Detienne, Marcel, *The Gardens of Adonis: Spices in Greek Mythology*, 2nd edn (Princeton: Princeton University Press, 2021)

Edmonds, Radcliffe, *Redefining Ancient Orphism: A Study in Greek Religion* (Cambridge University Press, 2013)

Edmonds III, Radcliffe G., 'Extra-Ordinary People: Mystai and Magoi, Magicians and Orphics in the Derveni Papyrus', *Classical Philology*, 103.1 (2008), 16-39

Faber, G. S., *A Dissertation on the Mysteries of the Cabiri: Or, The Great Gods of Phenicia, Samothrace, Egypt, Troas, Greece, Italy, and Crete; Being an Attempt to Deduce the Several Orgies of Isis, Ceres, Mithras, Bacchus, Rhea, Adonis, and Hecate, from a Union of the Rites Commemorative of the Deluge with the Adoration of the Hosts of Heaven*, Volume 2 (Oxford University Press, 1803)

Flaccus, Valerius, *Argonautica*, trans. by Mozley, 1.574

Graf, Fritz and Sarah Iles Johnston, *Ritual Texts for the Afterlife: Orpheus and the Bacchic Gold Tables* (Routledge, 2007)

Graf, Fritz, 'Serious Singing: The Orphic Hymns as Religious Texts,' *Kernos*, 22 (2009), 169-182

Hansen, Casper Worm, Peter Jensen, and Christian Volmar Skovsgaard, 'Gender Roles And Agricultural History: The Neolithic Inheritance', *Business History eJournal*, (2012), <https://pdfs.semanticscholar.org/acac/6ede1b35492215f07824c05c01a824dc467c.pdf>

Harrison, Jane Ellen, *Prolegomena to the Study of Greek Religion*, 3rd edn,(New York: The Noonday Press, 1955)

Harrison, Jane Ellen, *Themis: A Study of the Social Origins of Greek Religion* (Cambridge University Press, 2010)

'Hermes' Wondrous Victory Charm' in *The Greek Magical Papyri in Translation, Volume 1: Texts* (Chicago: University of Chicago Press, 1996)

Hesiod, *Theogony*, ed.by M. L. West (Oxford: Clarendon Press, 1966)

Hesiod, 'Works and Days' in *Hesiod, The Homeric Hymns and Homerica*, trans. by Hugh G. Evelyn-White (Cambridge: Harvard University Press, 1914)

Flavius, Josephus, *The Antiquities of the Jews* (N.p.: Wilder Publications, 2009)

Kerenyi, Karoly, *The Gods of the Greeks* (Hauraki Publishing, 2016)

Lillian B. Lawler, 'Two Notes on the Greek Dance', *The American Journal of Philology*, 69.1 (1948), 87–91 <https://doi.org/10.2307/291323>

Lyons, Deborah, *Gender and Immortality: Heroines in Ancient Greek Myth and Cult* (Princeton University Press, 2014)

Meisner, Dwayne, *Orphic Tradition and the Birth of the Gods* (Oxford University Press, 2018)

Nilsson, Martin, *Greek Folk Religion* (University of Pennsylvania Press, 1972)

Nonnus, *Dionysiaca*

Omitowoju, Rosanna, *Rape and the Politics of Consent in Classical Athens* (Cambridge University Press, 2002)

Orpheus, *The Mystical Hymns of Orpheus*, trans. by Thomas Taylor (United Kingdom: C. Whittingham, 1824)

Pausanias, *Description of Greece: A Pausanias Reader*, trans. by Gregory Nagy, (2020), *The Center for Hellenic Studies*, <https://chs.harvard.edu/description-of-greece-a-pausanias-reader/> [accessed 30 July 2022]

Pindar, *Odes*, ed. by Diane Arnson Svarlien, (1990), *Perseus*, <http://data.perseus.org/citations/urn:cts:greekLit:tlg0033.tlg002.perseus-eng1:11>

Plato, 'Phaedrus' in *Plato in Twelve Volumes*, 1, trans. by Harold North Fowler (Cambridge: Harvard University Press, 1914)

Richardson, N. J., 'The Orphic Poems', *The Classical Review*, 35.1 (1985), 87-90 <www.jstor.org/stable/3063696>

Robertson, Noel, 'Poseidon's Festival at the Winter Solstice', *The Classical Quarterly*, 34.1 (1984)

Room, Adrian, *NTC Classical Dictionary: the Origins of the Names of Characters in Classical Mythology and Literature* (National Textbook Company, 1990)

Siculus, Diodorus, *Library of History*

Tierney, Michael, 'A New Ritual of the Orphic Mysteries', The Classical Quarterly, 16.2 (1922), 77-87 <doi:10.1017/S0009838800002068>

Ustinova, Yulia, *Caves and the Ancient Greek Mind: Descending Underground in the Search for Ultimate Truth* (Oxford University Press, 2009)

Vogliano, Achille, 'La Grande iscrizione bacchica del Metropolitan Museum', *American Journal of Archaeology*, 37.2 (1933), <https://doi.org/10.2307/498439>

Watmouth, J.R., *Orphism* (Cambridge University Press, 2015)

West, Martin L., *The Orphic Poems* (Oxford University Press, 1984)

West, M. L., 'Notes on the Orphic Hymns', *The Classical Quarterly*, 18.2 (1968), 288-96 <http://www.jstor.org/stable/638072>

White, K. D., 'The Sacred Grove: A Comparative Study of Some Parallel Aspects of Religious Ritual in Ancient Crete and the Near East', *Greece & Rome*, 1.3 (1954), 112-27 <http://www.jstor.org/stable/642149>

Sources used in individual hymns

Hekate

D'Este Sorita and David Rankine, *Hekate: Liminal Rites* (London: Avalonia, 2009)
Johnston, Sarah Iles, *Restless Dead: Encounters between the Living and the Dead in Ancient Greece* (University of California Press, 2013)

Kronos

Griffiths, J. Gwyn, 'Archaeology and Hesiod's Five Ages', *Journal of the History of Ideas*, 17.1 (1956), *JSTOR*, <https://doi.org/10.2307/2707688> [accessed 26 July 2022]

Titans

Bremmer, Jan, *Greek Religion and Culture, the Bible and the Ancient Near East* (Brill Academic Publishing, 2008)
Solmsen, Friedrich, 'The Two Near Eastern Sources of Hesiod', *Hermes*, 117.4 (1989), 413-22
West, M.L., 'Hesiod's Titans', *The Journal of Hellenic Studies*, 105 (1985), 174-75
West, M.L., *Theogony: edited with prolegomena and commentary* (Claredon Press, 1966)

Adonis

Detienne, Marcel, *The Gardens of Adonis: Spices in Greek Mythology* (Princeton University Press, 1994)

Leukothea

De Grummond, Nancy T., 'Moon over Pyrgi: Catha, an Etruscan Lunar Goddess?', *American Journal of Archaeology* 112.3 (2008), 419-28 <http://www.jstor.org/stable/20627480>
Farnell, Lewis R., 'Ino-Leukothea', *The Journal of Hellenic Studies*, 36 (1916), 36-44
Finkelberg, Margalit, 'Ino-Leukothea between East and West', Journal of Ancient New Eastern Religions, 6.1 (2006) <https://doi.org/10.1163/156921206780602672>
West, Emily, 'A Quartet of Graeco-Aryan Demi-goddesses: Leukothea, Eddothea, Ulupi, and Varga', *Journal of Indo-European Studies*, 38.1/2 (2010), 147-71

Nymphs

Ballentine, Floyd G., 'Some Phases of the Cult of the Nymphs', *Harvard Studies in Classical Philology*, 15 (1904), 77-119 <https://doi.org/10.2307/310497>

Hill, Dorothy Kent, 'Nymphs and Fountains', *Antike Kunst*, 17.2 (1974), 107-08 <http://www.jstor.org/stable/41318597>

Tyche

Metzler, Dieter, 'Mural Crowns in the Ancient Near East and Greece', *Yale University Art Gallery Bulletin* (1994), 76-85 <http://www.jstor.org/stable/40514504>

Mnemosyne

Janko, R., 'An Unnoticed MS of Orphic Hymns 76-7', *The Classical Quarterly*, 35.2. (1985), 518-20

CPSIA information can be obtained
at www.ICGtesting.com
Printed in the USA
JSHW050244200523
41983JS00002B/39